Buddhism

Buddhism

A historical introduction to
Buddhist values and the social
and political forms they have
assumed in Asia

❧ ❧

PETER A. PARDUE

The Macmillan Company, New York, New York

Collier-Macmillan Limited, London

The Macmillan Company
866 Third Avenue, New York, N.Y. 10022
Collier-Macmillan Canada Ltd., Toronto, Ontario

Library of Congress
Catalog Card Number: 79-158931

First Macmillan Paperbacks Edition 1971

Printed in the United States of America

Portions of this book appeared earlier in *International
Encyclopedia of the Social Sciences* in the article
"Buddhism" by Peter A. Pardue.

Contents

Introduction

"BUDDHISM" is a Western term for the immensely diverse system of beliefs and practices centered on the teachings of the historical Buddha, who enunciated his message of salvation in India over two millennia ago. The general concept easily lends itself to a false sense of unity quite remote from the complex history of the tradition and the varied faiths of individual believers. India stands in a relationship to Asia which approximates that of ancient Hellenistic culture to the West—and the missionary bearer of its values was Buddhism. In the centuries following the promulgation of the original teaching and the formation of the earliest community, Indian Buddhism underwent a massive process of diffusion throughout the Asian world, assimilating new values and undergoing major changes in doctrine and institutions. Today, amid the acids of modernity, Buddhism, like all the great religions, finds itself subject to vast internal strains which further prohibit simplistic statements.

The traditional distinction between the major historical forms of Buddhism centers on a threefold typology, based on doctrinal and institutional differences which seem to fall within relatively homogeneous geographical areas. They are (1) The Theravāda ("teaching of the elders") located mainly in Ceylon and Indochina—most importantly in Burma, Thailand, Laos, and Cambodia; (2) the Mahāyāna ("great vehicle"), in Nepal, Sikkim, China, Korea, and Japan; and (3) the Tantrayāna ("esoteric vehicle"), formerly prevalent in Tibet, Mongolia, and parts of Siberia. However, this classification is crosscut with atypical variations. The Theravāda, as it exists today, represents the sole survivor of numerous ancient Indian schools. It has a fixed body of canonical literature, a relatively unified orthodox teaching, a clearly structured distinction between the monastic order and laity, and a long history as the established "church" of Ceylon and the major Indochinese states.

The Mahāyāna, on the other hand, is a diffuse and vastly complex combination of many schools and sects, based on a heterogeneous literature of massive proportions from which no uniform doctrinal or institutional orthodoxy can ever be derived. There are certain key scriptures which are sometimes regarded as typifying the more universal thrust of Mahāyāna principles over against Theravāda teaching, and Theravāda has traditionally been stigmatized as Hīnayāna ("small vehicle") by Mahāyānists; but Mahāyāna itself is also to be found on the Southeast Asian mainland, in syncretistic fusion with Theravāda and other indigenous media. Its literature ranges from the most abstruse philosophy to popular devotional theism and magic, and it includes the Hīnayāna sources as well. Institutionally it has appeared both in monastic and in radically laicized forms, and it has occasionally served in well-defined church-state configurations.

Tantric Buddhism, dominantly identified with Tibetan Lamaism and its theocracy, is equally ambiguous. The esoteric Tantric teachings, which originated in India, persisted in several so-called Mahāyāna schools in China and Japan and extended into Southeast Asia. In its Tibetan form Tantric Buddhism was richly fused with a native primitivism, and it underwent important and very divergent sectarian developments. The Tibetan monasteries contain (or did contain) superb collections of Mahāyāna and Hīnayāna sources in addition to the Tantric literature.

The statistics of Buddhist membership are even more deceptive. The total given has ranged from 100 million to 200 million—with the variation based principally on the fact that in Mahāyāna lands "orthodox" commitment to one religious faith was never a significant cultural characteristic. The populations of China and Japan could not be classed as Buddhist, Taoist, Confucian, or Shintōist in the same way that Western religious history seems to lend itself to relatively clear confessional divisions among Protestants, Catholics, and Jews. In Japan, for example, Buddhism, Confucianism, and Shintō have frequently formed a single interlocking system covering a wide range of personal and social needs. The same family that takes an infant to a Shintō shrine for a baptismal ceremony will, without any sense of conflict, have funeral rites conducted by Buddhist monks and maintain family ancestral worship and ethical standards largely dominated by Confucian values.

In Ceylon and the major Indochinese states, the great majority of the population have traditionally been Buddhist; but in China, just prior to the Communist takeover in 1949, less than 10 percent of the total population were specifically affiliated with the temples and monastic orders. Since 1949 this percentage has been drastically reduced, as it also has most recently in Tibet, where over one-fifth of the population once lived in the feudal monasteries, and the whole society was a Buddhist ecclesia. In Japan more than three-quarters of the population have had Buddhist affiliations, while in India and Pakistan—after an absence of many centuries—Buddhism has only recently begun to return in strength; but professing Buddhists are still a tiny minority, considerably less than 1 percent.

In the West, since the eighteenth century, with the first colonial input of Asian traditions and subsequent immigrations, Buddhism has found its way into Europe, Great Britain, South America, and the United States. The number of conversions among the native populations has been small; but much more significant has been the increasingly pervasive influence of Indian religious culture at many levels, often reflecting deep dissatisfaction with Western values and goals.

Amid this diversity are a few central elements that may be taken as generally characteristic of Buddhism throughout the larger part of its history. First, for all Buddhists the common point of unity has been in the symbol of the Buddha—whether revered chiefly as a human teacher or worshiped as a supreme deity. In all cases the element of personal commitment has been present in some form. Second, Buddhism is one of the three major religions of the world which incorporates all mankind within the scope of its universal message of salvation without prior criteria of social, ethnic, or geographic origin. The voluntary act of personal conversion in response to the teaching was, from the very beginning and still remains, one of the most decisive symbols of its missionary scope. Third, from the beginning Buddhism was dominated by a religious elite for whom the essential teaching demanded ardent pursuit of a mystical, otherworldly goal as an overriding concern— frequently to the exclusion of systematic focus on mundane socioeconomic and political problems. However, there have been many exceptions to this, which require that Buddhism be "defined" with careful regard for its discrete historical forms.

In various ways, it has been said of Buddhism, that no religion or mystical philosophy which has so radically affirmed the illusory character and anguish of existence and sought release from it, has at the same time so often had the everyday world thrust upon it. The apparently "irrational" consequences of Buddhist values in their articulation with economic and political structures have been explored classically by Max Weber.[1] He characterized Buddhism as an "other-worldly mysticism" in polar contrast with the "inner-worldly asceticism" distilled out of the Judeo-Christian tradition, most potently in its Calvinist form—seeking mastery over the world and maximization of economic power and political controls as an expression of an inward ascetic calling. Subsequent studies of particular historical adaptations of Buddhism to the cultural and institutional needs of the Asian states have provided both interesting confirmations and important qualifications of this thesis.[2]

Moreover, it was not Weber's goal to denigrate Buddhism or the various forms of Indian and East Asian spirituality—although he has often been interpreted this way. A central aspect of his work was to point directly to a massive historical irony: the technological, economic, and scientific transformation of Western European civilization —closely related to special configurations of Judeo-Christian and Hellenistic values—was combined with dehumanizing irrationalities, political brutalization, and the corrosion of the spiritual principles from which this power had, in part, sprung. Hence his famous and deeply pessimistic prophecy at the end of *The Protestant Ethic*: "For the last stage of this cultural development it might well be truly said: 'specialists without spirit, sensualists without heart; this nullity imagines that it has attained a level of civilization never before achieved.' "[3] He did not try to predict which if any of the great religions, or in what transformation, might in the end prove to be most vital and "relevant" to human self-understanding and social reconstruction.

Buddhism has evidenced from the very beginning a deep commitment to the exploration of the mystery and meaning of the self amid the finite conditions of human life and the transience of all worldly forms to which man has compulsively attributed ultimate worth. The paradoxa of illusion and reality, of anxious human striving in the world and the longing for withdrawal from it, of dogmatic ethical imperatives and their merely provisional conditions—all these have been richly elaborated within a prognostic framework which has had a profound impact on the great Asian civilizations, and which now reaches deeply into the matrix of Western culture.

Our aim in the following pages is to examine some of the historical relationships—from the ancient to the modern period—between these basic values and the diverse cultural, social, and political forms in which they have been expressed and taken root.

Buddhism

1. India

THE CONDITIONS underlying the emergence of Buddhism in ancient India were generally characteristic of a wider process of sociocultural transition which took place during the first millennium B.C. across the face of the civilized world, from Greece to China. In the great centers of high culture, archaic social and religious institutions were breaking down under the pressure of the more complex forms of economic and political activity associated with the later phases of the urban revolution and the territorial expansion of new imperial states. These fundamental changes in the physical conditions of existence not only fractured old cultural and political boundaries; they created the urgent need for new values and forms of human solidarity, and at the same time made possible these developments. In each case economic and political advances were mixed with serious social disorders, hardship, and the loss of traditional religious moorings.

In this process, new philosophical and religious solutions were sought by thinkers whose teachings lie behind the major civilizations of the world today. Socrates, the

prophets of Israel, Confucius, and the Buddha were among
the great innovators, who, in distinctive ways, offered
critiques of the older values and redefined the meaning of
existence and the nature of man and society within a more
universal, transcendent framework which became the basis
for long-range reconstruction.[1]

The archaic cultural and social matrix of India was
shaped under the influence of Āryan civilization in synthesis with native traditions. In the second millennium B.C.
the Āryan tribes had penetrated the subcontinent, carry-
ing with them the rudiments of a prehistoric culture, the
traces of which remained in a common heritage stretching
from Greece through Iran into India. Their religious and
social institutions were centered around a highly articulate
sacrificial cult embodied in the *Veda*, and were grounded
on a priestly and warrior aristocracy who controlled the
principal means of legitimation and political authority.
Cultic symbols were comprised of a rich mythological and
ritual system focused on a pantheon of high gods personi-
fying the sacred forces of the universe and sanctifying
Āryan social norms. As the tribes settled in permanent
agricultural communities, the cult evolved into an elaborate technocracy in which the *Brāhman* priesthood gradually accumulated immense ritual and social power. They
provided the sacred rationale for the classical caste system,
finally forming the top echelon of the hierarchy which was
further differentiated into hereditary subcastes. The in-
crement in priestly authority was the result of essential
services performed in behalf of Āryan religious needs,
solidarity, and diffusion—particularly the legitimation of
the warrior elite. But it was also the result of the continuous rationalization of primary cultic symbols, driving
toward a monistic conception of the sacred source of all
phenomena over which the priestly sciences exercised de-

terminative ritual control. Speculative innovations were essential to the larger process, and the Vedic literature itself is a remarkable testimony to this "evolutionary" development.[2]

By the seventh and six centuries B.C. many areas in northern India were under the influence of Āryan culture even in the absence of direct political authority. However, the old Āryan cult and social system were subject to countervailing pressures. At the economic and political level there were significant developments in urban commerce based on a money economy, the beginnings of rational bureaucracy, and a new and increasingly affluent middle class. In addition there were protracted wars between newly emerging states and petty kingdoms for control of territory and economic resources. These power struggles resulted in the uprooting and extirpation of political minorities and the corrosion of the old forms of communal solidarity and legitimation. As the archaic means for maintaining religious and social integration dissolved, the situation provoked a deep spiritual malaise which intensified earlier speculations about the meaning of the self and the world. The value of all traditional worldly forms and of life itself was called into question with unparalleled sharpness.

Some of the cultural resources for this massive critique may have come from an old indigenous religious tradition developed by an intellectual elite who rejected the archaic sacrificial cult and its worldly goals in favor of meditational and ascetic disciplines leading to personal spiritual mastery and mystical experience. The alignment of this elite with economic and political groups who chafed under Āryan social controls is also possible; but prior to the sixth century, the historical evidence for this is slim.

The new religious and philosophical teachers of this era —most significantly those whose doctrines are embodied in the *Upaniṣads,* in Buddhism, and in Jainism—began their reconstructive enterprise with a radical devaluation of the external forms of the phenomenal world; they affirmed an otherworldly realm of absolute transcendence which alone is worthy to be the goal of religious striving, and is the consequence of inward mental and spiritual self-perfection—not of external rites.

Furthermore, many of the new schools appropriated a transmigrational metaphysic which forms an almost airtight theodicy. The rudiments of this teaching define the normative religious problem as one of personal salvation from bondage to phenomenal existence: the soul (*ātman*) undergoes an endless cycle of rebirths (*saṃsāra*), in which the individual assumes a new physical form and status in the next life depending on the quality of actions (*karma*) in this life. No worldly contingency is without rational cause. Ultimate salvation can be attained through a purifying, intuitive knowledge of the essential spiritual integrity of the self. Appropriate techniques were embodied classically in the *yoga*—an autonomous, often ascetic discipline of the mind, body, and inner motivations, designed to engender transforming mystical insight and to eliminate the karmic source of the transmigratory process.

These reforming movements penetrated the Āryan Vedic tradition and hastened speculative developments which culminated in the extraordinary literature of the Upaniṣads. Both the critical and the constructive goals of this era are echoed in one of the later texts:

Sacrificial rites are unstable boats [on the sea of life]. . . . The fools who regard them as the highest spiritual good go round and round in the cycle of old age and death. . . . But those who practice ascetic self-discipline become the tranquil ones who know the truth. . . . Free of passion they finally depart to immortality.[3]

This world-view was shared in a very rudimentary way by many new schools. Its most striking general characteristic is the emphasis on personal spiritual independence—clearly therapeutic in an era marked by social disintegration, the brutalization of life, and the decline of traditional religious certainties. It was even suggested that the gods themselves were subject to the transmigratory process, and hence mortal—theoretically rendering the great theistic cult only provisionally useful. This diverse and remarkably creative search for new models of reality during this "time of troubles" was driven by an overwhelming need to discriminate between the essential, lasting elements of man's nature—the true "self"—and the merely provisional conditions of its finite and anxiety-ridden existence. The new prognosis was centered on symbolic paradigms which affirmed the qualitative freedom of the self over the moribund conditions of the world and its transient forms; one which instilled a sense of personal identity unassailable by any external force whether it be death, the everyday vicissitudes of life, or the mediation of a priestly bureaucracy. Lines of religious authority were partly restructured to stress personal confrontation and maturing dialogue between the teacher and his disciples.

However, despite these generally shared goals, there were sharp sectarian disputes on theoretical particulars, and this conflict was heightened by disagreements over the prevalent theory of social stratification, the caste system. From the Brāhmanic perspective the Upaniṣads were an esoteric gnosis restricted to the Āryan elite. All means of salvation were contained in the Vedic lore, and the law of karma was tied rigidly to caste: one is born in a particular social station as a result of deeds in the former life, and conformity to caste rules is the precondition of salvation or at least of improvement in status in the next life.

In addition, the old sacrificial and magical cult persisted. The Brāhman student was urged to seek "a *guru* who is expert in the Vedic scriptures"—including both archaic rites and the secrets of the new teaching.

By contrast, the non-Brāhmanic schools like Buddhism and Jainism—though they were not basically social reforming movements—denied the ultimate sanctity of the Vedas, the religious superiority of the Brāhmans, and the ritual significance of caste. Their messages of salvation were preached openly. Admission was based on personal conversion, usually without ascriptive limits of caste, class, or sex. And it is not surprising, therefore, to find evidence that their teachings found rich soil among upwardly mobile urban commercial and political groups, who held that both religious and social standing should be based on personal talent and achievement rather than hereditary right. It is significant that, according to the traditions, both the Buddha and Mahāvīra—the founder of Jainism—were from indigenous non-Āryan tribes.

Efforts to reconstruct the life and teachings of the Buddha and the institutions of the earliest community run aground on many refractory critical problems.[4] The Buddha's life story appears in a number of versions of varying quality and is often immersed in myth, legend, and miracle. These embellishments, however, are historically important: they endow the human teacher and his doctrine with a paradigmatic sanctity which is an actual measurement of its importance and long-range historical impact; and they reflect mythopoeic presuppositions and forms of popular piety from which the community fashioned important dimensions of its symbolic and institutional life.

The rudimentary biographical details are at least plausible in general outline: the historical Buddha, named Siddhārtha Gautama, was born a prince of an old indigenous clan called the Śākyas in northern India about 560 B.C. In rank, the Śākyas were rated according to Āryan values as "warriors" (*Kṣatriyas*), that is, members of the nobility; however, their actual circumstances were relatively humble. They controlled the small village of Kapilavastu in the foothills of the Himalāyas but they were under the suzerainty of the powerful neighboring kingdom of Kosala. It is doubtful that they had substantive military or economic power. Clan institutions were principally oligarchical—with the elders serving as advisers to "King" Śuddhodana—the Buddha's father—who was little more than a local chief.

In his early youth Gautama was doubtless trained in the formal Kṣatriya arts of horsemanship and the techniques of war and kingship, and was also certainly exposed to the wider framework of Āryan culture. We can only speculate on the irrelevance of the warrior model and the archaic cult to the prince of a small enfiefed clan in an age of brutalizing warfare. Moreover, the tradition relates that he showed unusual sensitivity to the pressing enigmas of human existence. His father tried to distract him from these concerns. Gautama married and had a son. But at the age of twenty-nine, increasingly preoccupied with the classical problems of religious meaning, suffering, decay, and death, he left his family for systematic exploration of these perplexing issues. His departure—the "Great Renunciation"—conforms to the model of ascetic withdrawal and mendicancy which was an institutionally approved option for the mature householder who could not deny his inner religious commitments.

For a number of years he studied, tested, and subsequently rejected prevailing doctrines ranging from speculative philosophy and techniques of mystical trance to severe bodily self-mortification. Finally, in a single night of intensive meditation he achieved a decisive spiritual breakthrough—attaining a transforming wisdom (*prajñā*), enlightenment (*bodhi*), and the ineffable *nirvāṇa* (literally "blowing out")—a state of mystical transcendence beyond all conceptualization, signifying his victory over fear, death, the transmigratory process, and all forms of human finitude.

Some of the mythological and legendary materials present him as a supernatural being who chooses to be born miraculously at this pivotal time and place in human history. His life is attended with suitable portents, and his enlightenment is surrounded with a new cosmology in which the old gods and demons are subordinated to his spiritual powers. The Buddha is qualitatively above the gods because he has broken through and transcended the omnipotent law of karma to which they are subject despite their exalted status. This mythological "reform" was important because it established a new level of symbolic control in which many aspects of the archaic theistic cults were incorporated and yet transformed to reinforce the basic values of the teaching. Thereafter, as the Buddha ("enlightened one"), he evolved the main doctrinal components of his teaching (*Dharma*) and embarked on a missionary career, preaching his new discovery openly to all "without a closed fist."[5] He formed an ever-widening community (*Saṅgha*) of mendicant disciples from all castes, including women and lay devotees, and after a long ministry he died at the age of eighty.

The earliest traditions represent the Buddha as teaching an exoteric, practical yoga of almost Cartesian simplicity, though in fact it is loaded with philosophical problems which provided a rich source for later doctrinal and institutional elaboration. In a sense, the subsequent history of Buddhism centers on the possibilities for exploring the implications of the teaching developed in articulation with the immense spectrum of discrete human needs, institutions, and cultures with which it was brought into contact.

The general form of the teaching is called the "Middle Path." It is a mean between the extremes of bodily self-indulgence and self-mortification. This is a qualitative, not merely an expedient mean. It is based on the conviction that extreme physical mortification is no more than an ironic inversion of bodily self-indulgence, since both focus on the external physical form and do not touch the real core of the human problem, namely, the habitual errors of the mind and the inward perversion of the will and motivations. For the same reason both speculative philosophy and the old sacrificial cults are wide off the mark, because they do not center directly on the inner sources of mental habituation, irrational impulse, and behavior.

The Buddha's specific diagnosis of the human situation and his method of salvation are stated classically in the Four Noble Truths which we present here in synopsis drawn from Theravādin tradition. The shortest form, among many in which they appear, is simply: "This is Sorrow; this is the Cause of Sorrow; this is the Cessation of Sorrow; this is the Way leading to the Cessation of Sorrow."[6] In fuller exposition: (1) All creaturely existence is marked by suffering, sorrow, pain (*dukkha*), an agonized bondage to the meaningless cycle of birth and death amid a transitory flux which is momentary, impermanent (*anicca*) and without essential being (*anattā*: literally "no-soul"). (2) The principal cause of this condition is profound ignorance (*avijjā*) of the illusory nature of the phenomenal world which engenders uncontrollable desires or craving (*taṇhā*) for transient entities—the mistaken attribution of ultimate worth to finite forms which come into being only to decay and dissolve. Particularly pernicious is the notion of the eternality of soul; it is a phenomenal construct—a combination of rudimentary mental, psychophysical, and sensory forms. The desire for continued personal existence beyond its finite "composite" conditions is not only the source of delusion and paralyzing fear, but has an even more dreadful consequence: as the individual soul begins to dissolve in death, the subtle craving for existence binds the phenomenal elements together once again and, in an inexorable causal sequence, chains it to the cycle of rebirth and suffering. (3) The elimination of ignorance about the illusory nature of phenomenal things and the extirpation of egregious craving for them will break the causal sequence and so precipitate final salvation. (4) For this purpose the appropriate yoga is the Eightfold Path, an integral combination of ethical and meditational disciplines which jointly purify the motivations and the mind. This leads in turn to the attainment of a final state of spiritual perfection marked by threshold mystical experiences culminating in final enlightenment and release, that is, *nibbāna* (nirvāṇa).

The rudiments of the teaching outlined here can give only the barest suggestion of its innovative and therapeutic power. Always foremost is the paradigmatic grandeur of spiritual transcendence, renewal, and maturation represented by the Buddha himself. His ascetic withdrawal from the givenness of the everyday world and his negation of it is the first step in gaining new critical leverage over it. These symbols of world rejection and negation are not pessimistic or nihilistic. They "negate" the distorted values which enslave the personality to inner compulsions and which render the individual a helpless victim of his own insatiable appetites. They place the broken and disrupted forms of the external world in critical perspective, and undercut the old institutional dependencies—especially the reliance on primitive and archaic religious practices, magic, and external rites. The yoga is the autonomous work of the self-reliant individual who performs the "inward" sacrifice. His welfare and spiritual transformation are in his own hands. Hence the teaching is profoundly optimistic. The early sources are rich in materials which express this sense of liberation:

> When men are afraid, they often seek refuge in [the spirits of] the hills, woods, gardens, trees and shrines. . . . But this refuge offers no security. . . . Whoever seeks refuge in the Noble Truths, and with wisdom sees [the truths of] sorrow, its origin, its cessation, and the noble eightfold path that leads to victory, only such a man is set free.[7]

Freedom is a direct consequence of the fact that all causal forces and techniques of control effecting the fate of man are internalized. The basic theory of causation embedded in the second Truth is called "dependent origination" (*paṭiccasamuppāda*, "this given, that arises"); and the causal sequences, or "chains" (*nidāna*), of the rebirth process are given in one formulation as follows:

> Ignorance is the cause of psychic constructions, hence is caused consciousness, physical form, the senses, contact, sensations, craving, attachment, becoming, and so birth, old age and death with all the distraction of grief, lamentation, sorrow and despair.[8]

The perfected disciple has unqualified control over this causal chain, especially over the two key links: ignorance and craving. He cannot, therefore, be victimized by any agent other than himself.

Furthermore the anattā doctrine had an equally positive valence despite its "negative" appearance: first, it overtly incorporated and placed within a positive system of salvation a pervasive skepticism about theories which affirmed the eternality of the soul—a position held in both Jain and

Brāhmanic teachings but denied by some materialist schools. Second, it removed the last vestige of an external cosmology which asserted that the soul had an eternal and necessary (hence fated) relationship to some extrinsic overarching force or sacred entity—to the gods, an ultimate "spirit," heaven, or the law of karma. Thus the paradoxical conviction that the final obliteration of the finite self is an infinitely desirable mystical experience had the remarkable psychological advantage of reinforcing a model of radical freedom and transcendence without equal in any other teaching.

With respect to ethical and social reconstruction, the apparent deprecation of the phenomenal world, its given values and forms, had the potential to cut through old provincial values and institutions, and to place all men in a universal context of meaning through which the whole human situation could be comprehended and managed. Correlatively, it was possible to inculcate universal standards of conduct which establish expectations of interpersonal and intergroup relationships without limits.

The initial act of conversion, expressed in commitment to the "Buddha, Dharma, and Saṅgha," not only allows for the dramatization of personal dissatisfaction with one's present life situation, but projects a long-range program of spiritual recovery and maturation, and the internalization of new values, which can be publicly acted out. Enlightenment is not only the result of incessant meditation on the Noble Truths and on the transitoriness of life, which will ultimately eradicate desire for it; it requires motivational purification through the practice of universal virtues in addition to monastic poverty and continence: love and compassion toward all living creatures, the elimination of a host of specific vices "and all inclinations to them," and the obligation to promote friendship and concord. Within the community, ideally, the ritual divisions of caste and worldly social conventions are obliterated before the universal force of love and the knowledge of the common condition of mankind.

The Eightfold Path combines ethics and meditational discipline in an interesting way. The traditional scheme presents the eight steps sequentially: "right views, intention, speech, action, livelihood, effort, mindfulness, and concentration," which are sometimes further reduced to three principles: wisdom, morality, and meditation. "Right views and intention" signify knowledge of and commitment to the Buddha's Dharma. But to know the Dharma in depth demands massive cognitive and cathectic changes through an intensive effort of the will, continual reflection, reinforcement, and incorporation of the symbolic pattern until it has become constitutive of the whole personality. Only then is simple knowledge transformed into salutary wisdom. In this process, the moral requirements (speech, action, livelihood) seem at first to be narrowly functional, consisting of negative and positive injunctions suited to ethical probity and social interaction; they are presented as obligatory goals of conscious striving (noninjury, no lying, humility, etc.). But these ethical imperatives also serve to block impulsive, uncontrolled thought and behavior for the larger purpose of providing a stable psychic base for focused meditation on the Truths. They lose their coercive quality and become increasingly the positive expression of inward mastery and exaltation. The coordination of moral discipline and meditation on the Truths for building a fixed state of purified consciousness is expressed in the following passage on the four "cardinal" virtues in the teaching on "Right Mindfulness."

Develop the state of mind of love (*mettā*), . . . for as you do hostility will grow less; and of compassion (*karuṇā*), for anxiety will grow less; and of joy (*muditā*), for aversion will grow less; and of equanimity (*upekkhā*), for repugnance will grow less.

And develop a consciousness of the corruption of the body, for
thus passion will grow less; and develop a consciousness of the
impermanence of all things, for thus the pride of self-hood will
grow less.[9]

The acquisition of these supreme virtues reflects the dissolution of the ego-boundary through "unlimited," loving
inclusion of other sentient creatures, and the dropping
away of the behavioral stigma of "I-ness" (hostility, aversion, pride, etc.), which in turn signifies large-scale spiritual maturation. In the end, systematic contemplation on
the illusoriness of all phenomena combined with these
moral perfections culminates in a qualitative disentangle-
ment from all finite and conditioned things and an approach to the "unconditioned"—"the doors of the undying"
—nirvāṇa. Ultimate liberation comes with death itself
(*parinirvāṇa*, "total extinction"), the external physical event
which secures the final reward of completed spiritual perfection.

Despite its exoteric simplicity, methodical structure, and
ethical universalism, the teaching was in many respects
deeply problematical. It may be helpful, here, to outline
a few of the major dilemmas around which subsequent
institutional and doctrinal controversies developed. First,
the teaching did not aim to provide "rational" means for
social reform or therapeutic adjustments to everyday life.
It was driven by a categorical affirmation of the value of
personal salvation as an end in itself—an odyssey of systematic withdrawal from the illusory snares of the world.
Ascription of real worth and meaning to the phenomenal
world is the source of craving and the most egregious
errors.

Second, the Dharma demands total commitment adequately expressed only in the role of the mendicant monk
who has abandoned the aspirations of the everyday world

and has devoted his life to full-time pursuit of salvation. Although the lay householder might practice the yoga and originally was not excluded from the mystical goal (the Buddha said only that it was "harder" for the laity to attain nirvāṇa), it was inevitable that the ideal of full spiritual perfection should be reserved for those whose deeper concern was institutionally defined by complete monastic commitment. Consequently, the spiritual status of the laity was from the beginning subject to many uncertainties.

Third, the anattā doctrine and the affirmation of the transient character of all phenomena raised the problem of validating human relationships and ethical interaction. How can there be any meaningful relationship between illusory manifestations, human or otherwise? And on what grounds is it possible to justify normative standards or ethics without an ontology or an affirmation of essential being which establishes their ultimate worth?

Fourth, the Buddha is represented as rejecting teachings which affirmed either that the elements of all phenomena exist eternally or do not, and indeed as rejecting all purely speculative matters of this sort, calling them "indeterminant, . . . not leading to enlightenment," since they distorted the yoga in the direction of compulsive intellection. Yet the classical philosophical questions persisted: the source and structure of illusion itself, of being and nonbeing; the validation of perception and knowledge—these issues and many more were, as in Brāhmanic philosophy, unavoidable problems with which many Buddhist intellectuals felt compelled to struggle in subsequent generations.

Fifth, nirvāṇa is a supreme mystical goal the inherent integrity of which is partly dependent on the fact that it cannot be represented through spatio-temporal media. It is not a transcendent entity like the Upaniṣadic *Brahman,* even though it is often described positively as a joyous state of mystical transcendence and bliss. The Buddha is occasionally represented as describing it negatively as "pathless," "void," or paradoxically as beyond all subject-object polarities, or even more saliently by his silence. A particularly revealing legend relates that after his enlightenment he doubted that it would be possible to communicate his experience to others, and was only persuaded to do so after the great Hindu god Brahmā appeared to plead that he undertake the arduous task out of compassion for his fellow men and his knowledge that some of them were bright enough to understand. In general the symbolism is managed to heighten and dramatize the indecipherable qualities of final liberation. Moreover, to speak of nirvāṇa as a goal at all entailed a massive irony: if nirvāṇa is an otherworldly goal to be attained as a reward of the yoga, it is a *desirable* goal. The monk, therefore, is fated to be the victim of craving in this subtle form, and so in the end cannot escape the very thing he strives to overcome. Furthermore, if consciousness—the persisting element of ego-identity—dissolves at death, what is left to "experience" either karmic transmigration or nirvāṇa?

Some of the early texts reflect controversies which developed during the Buddha's own lifetime precisely on these issues. In one sermon he is represented as excoriating a "stupid" monk for his obdurate misunderstanding of the teaching on this count. The text concludes with a remarkable passage which holds these problems in paradoxical tension, though it does not resolve them:

[The enlightened monk] clings to nothing in the world; and not clinging he does not tremble, and not trembling he attains nibbāna. . . . It would be absurd to say of such a monk, with his heart set free, that he believes the perfected being survives, or that he does and yet does not, or that he neither does nor does not. Because the monk is free, therefore his state transcends all expression, predication, communication, and knowledge.[10]

In this framework there is a pragmatic validation of the positive psychological benefits of spiritual perfection, namely, freedom from anxiety and fear; and at the same time there is the assertion that the ultimate condition of liberation is beyond all verbal or conceptual dichotomies.

It is important to realize that none of these doctrinal antinomies worked to the disadvantage of the missionary movement—rather, quite the reverse. There is a genuine atmosphere of esotericism and profundity which is redolent of immensely rich areas for exploration—all within the microcosm of the self. The growth of the community and the development of the early schools—some eighteen to twenty in number—were in part the result of sectarian disagreements among the intellectual elite, on these and other problems embedded in the earliest teaching, as they strove for clarification, spiritual mastery, and prestige.

As we trace the institutional development of the earliest community against the background of these endemic problems, we find it centered at first around the charisma and teaching of the Buddha himself. But the growing number of converts, the addition of lay devotees and the settlement of coenobitic communities around major cities in the Ganges valley forced the routinization of communal life. By the end of the Buddha's long ministry the Saṅgha was differentiated along several characteristic lines; most important was the two-class distinction between the monastic elite and the lay devotees.

Since the laity did not share in the rigor of the full monastic life, it could not—except in rare cases—aspire to the benefits of the ultimate spiritual goal. The hardening of this line of demarcation appears subtly in a number of formulations:

> The man whose mind is preoccupied
> with the welfare of children and herds,
> is overwhelmed by death as a
> slumbering village by a great flood.[11]

This was asserted more strongly in the representative conviction that "there can be no perfected man outside the monastic order." Nevertheless, characteristic institutional and religious adjustments were made: for the laity, there was a secondary method of salvation based on a merit-making ethic. In joining the Saṅgha, the lay devotees promised to conform to the "five precepts": no killing, stealing, lying, adultery, or alcoholic beverages (the last was occasionally deleted from the list). And by their support of the monastic order through personal piety, giving food and other gifts, they could accumulate karmic merit and so be assured of better rebirth opportunities. This was regarded as a lower and somewhat worldly aim, since desire for a better rebirth did little more than perpetuate craving for existence. But even so, the lay ethic was not developed casually. The laity were integral members of the community; their life-style reflected directly on the probity and spiritual values of the monastic order, and from their ranks came new monastic recruits already educated in the basic teachings.

Subsequent institutional developments followed a number of lines. The tradition states that after the Buddha's death a council was convened at the city of Rājagṛha to regularize the teachings and monastic rule.[12] The actual accomplishments of the council are uncertain, but it is probable that some of the major scriptures found in the present Theravādin canon and the residuals of other early schools already existed in oral form, including the nuclear disciplinary code (*Prātimokṣa*) of the later full monastic rule (*Vinaya*) and many of the teachings embodied in the Buddha's discourses (*Sūtra*). The major ceremonials of communal life were in practice, most importantly the bimonthly confessional "observance"—*uposatha* (*poṣadha*) a congregational assembly and recital of the Prātimokṣa.

This early code in its Theravādin form consists of some 227 rules governing monastic life, and ranging from major offenses requiring expulsion from the order to minor rules concerning daily personal demeanor and procedural matters.[13] The four major offenses for which no expiation was possible were (1) sexual intercourse, (2) stealing, (3) killing a human being or inciting to suicide, and (4) falsely claiming supernatural powers. Sexual prohibitions were spelled out in detail: they highlighted the spiritual model of complete devotion to the Dharma and the ascetic value of denying one of the strongest instinctual drives; and they validated deeply rooted taboos, including all acts associated with procreation and the fated impurities of the cycle of birth and death. They were also related to the old and prevalent ascetic notion that release of sexual energies impaired the accumulation of the necessary strength for spiritual striving. Perhaps equally important was the fact that sexual activity was specifically "antisocial" in that it disrupted the shared values essential to communal solidarity just as surely as murder or theft.

Aspects of the problem of sexuality are reflected in the traditions which tell how the Order of Nuns was established. The Buddha was reluctant to allow this innovation despite his formal recognition that women were fully capable of spiritual perfection. When he finally agreed, he is represented as having predicted that the health and longevity of the Dharma would be greatly impaired. The nuns were subordinated to the superior status of the monks, and the rules governing their monastic life were even more detailed and restrictive. Both the residuals of the old patriarchal tradition and the latent fear of sexual provocation seem to lie at the heart of this tradition. In general, however, it is noteworthy that the monastic rules were singularly free of the archaic taboos concerning food and other magical impurities which characterize the religious laws of traditional Hinduism, Zoroastrianism, and ancient Hebrew tradition.

The prohibition against false claims to supernatural powers is especially interesting: the Buddha and other early saints were presumed to have attained a number of superhuman skills at the moment of enlightenment, including omniscience, clairvoyance, and the power of magical flight. In the Saṅgha, a premature claim of this sort could be immensely disruptive because it violated the communal integrity and expectations predicated on a long period of spiritual discipline before these skills could be attained. Perfected monks were forbidden to boast about these powers even if they had them.

Other serious offenses centered around acts which disrupted communal concord: gossip, quarreling, slander, or having personal property in excess of the minimum allowed. Minor rules of personal deportment, politeness, and etiquette are also spelled out in detail. They served to civilize the rude novice in manners appropriate to everyday monastic amenities and the public image of the Saṅgha; and they were the basis for more advanced study in the Dharma with an elder teacher. Rules governing admission to the Saṅgha excluded debtors, fugitives, those without parental permission, and those with severe diseases or bodily defects. It is apparent that these restrictions were intended both to minimize public criticism and to protect the community against undesirables, since obviously the motives for joining the monastic order could be seriously distorted. In addition, the novice was not admitted to full ordination until his sincerity had been extensively observed and tested.

The monk was forbidden to cultivate the soil, possess money, or engage in trade—all of which could lead to preoccupation with worldly affairs. Lay devotees were often assigned the task of managing the economic and physical properties of the Saṅgha, and even enforcing internal discipline where monastic procedures failed. Despite its restrictive character, in general the Prātimokṣa conveys an image of vital communal life reflecting the deep need and real pleasures of mutual support in the study of the Dharma.

The fellowship of the monastic life itself is represented as one filled with a profound satisfaction in the higher calling and privileged spiritual status:

> Joyful is the coming of the Buddhas.
> Joyful is the guidance of the Dharma.
> Joyful is the concord of the Saṅgha.
> Joyful is the austere life of those at one.[14]

It is notable that the rule against inciting to suicide (by saying, for example, "Ho, man, what is this evil life to thee?") is directed against those who disrupt this mood of exaltation and promote the "craving" for simple self-annihilation—a gross delusion which sends the individual back into the rebirth cycle. To be born as a human being among all the various species of sentient creatures and lower forms of life was a great event. It afforded a rare opportunity amid many transmigrations to practice the Buddha's teaching. Consequently, human life had great dignity and worth.

One of the most important monastic rules required that

the monk obtain food and other bare necessities by beg-
ging. Mendicancy was not only an appropriate traditional
model of asceticism and poverty, it had a number of positive functions: first, it expressed the spiritual independence
of the monk, his nonattachment to worldly fixtures and his
wholehearted commitment to the Dharma. Second, it was
an exercise in humility, since he was obliged to accept
what was given him without complaint. Third, the act of
"giving" (*dāna*) was the central ritual means through
which the laity could earn spiritual merit, and was often
the occasion for preaching the Dharma. Fourth, by the
deliberate act of refusing to accept alms, it was a powerful
medium for disciplining reprobates who were thus publicly stigmatized; and this procedure could be reversed:
the laity could refuse to give alms to an unworthy monk.

However, this institution was vulnerable to excessive
charity. As with some of the great ascetic orders of the
medieval Christian church, the generosity of the laity
slowly undermined the rigor of the early mendicant tradition. Some of the monastic centers acquired extensive
properties and economic resources which demanded a
highly differentiated administrative system. These worldly
accommodations apparently monopolized an increasingly
large sector of monastic life and attracted drones, which
in turn provoked complaints and schism even during the
Buddha's own lifetime. His cousin Devadatta is reputed
to have attempted to gain control of the Order in the
name of a more rigorous ascetic standard. Though it is
difficult to ascertain the actual facts behind this story, it
reflects aspects of the larger process of schism and sectarian development out of the conflict over the teaching
and monastic rules.

The doctrinal dilemmas cited above were exacerbated
by geographical and provincial differences, and inevitably

by the emergence of distinguished "elders" with divergent
views as to the meaning of the more problematical teachings. With respect to the quandaries of the anattā doctrine
and other illusionist propositions, we find one sect, the Pud-
galavāda, teaching that the essential "person" (*pudgala*)
persists after death. This position was later declared
heretical by the Theravāda, which nevertheless developed
its own subtle metaphysical continuum, the *bhāvanga* (essential "part of becoming")—a kind of living subconscious
persisting in the stream of impermanence. Another of the
most important and long-lived early sects, the Sarvāstivāda
(the "doctrine that everything exists"), dealt with the problem of illusion and reality by asserting that all transient
phenomena subsist in an atomic pluralism of compounded
forms with exception of the most rudimentary elements—
including nirvāṇa itself—which is essentially pure and
"uncompounded."

As the sects evolved into formal schools their distinctive
doctrinal positions were embodied in elaborate scholastic
commentaries on the Buddha's sermons, finally forming—
to take the Theravādin case— the *Abhidhamma* ("on the
doctrine"), which is the third part of the threefold canon
(*Tipiṭaka*, literally "three baskets"); the first two parts
consist of the Buddha's sermons and the monastic rule.
According to tradition, a second council was convened at
the city of Vaiśālī one hundred years after the Buddha's
death. There a series of sharp disagreements about the
inner meaning of the teaching, the status of the laity, and
the rigors of the monastic rule brought on a major schism
chiefly between the forerunners of the Theravāda and the
more liberal Mahāsaṅghika ("Great Saṅgha") whose doctrines were related to the rise of Mahāyāna Buddhism in
the following centuries.[15]

The apparent failure of the first councils to unite the

Saṅgha has to be gauged against the basic values of the
teaching itself, the nature of the monastic constitution, and
the concept of authority. The early Saṅgha was never a
"church" under one centralized control or subscriptionist
orthodoxy. At Rājagṛha, after the Buddha's death and sup-
posedly at his own request, the idea of routine patriarchal
succession was deliberately rejected.[16] The primary function of the monastic rule was to protect the spiritual
independence of each monk and to provide optimum conditions for pursuit of the ultimate religious goal, not to
enforce ecclesiastical unity. Issues were discussed openly
and decided by majority vote, with all ordained monks
having equal franchise. The monastic rules governing internal disagreements allowed free dissent in "good faith,"
and if controversies could not be resolved, the rules allowed the dissenters to depart and form their own monastic
center. Formal routinization of internal authority finally
included a status system based upon degrees of spiritual
perfection, knowledge and capacity to instruct, and
seniority reckoned in a sequence of three decades from
the date of ordination. There was a preceptor system for
the guidance of novice monks, but the authority of the
senior monks was in principle strictly advisory. The novice
joined the Saṅgha by confessing his inward spiritual intention, but not within a system of bureaucratic authority
as in the Roman and Byzantine churches, or of monastic
obedience such as we find in the Benedictine Rule.

In fact, the monastic rule in the Prātimokṣa and later
Vinaya was always something of an anomaly. In its earliest
form it was probably not a disciplinary code but, rather,
a personal confession of faith and ethical intention. Its
identification with regulatory prescriptions and penalties
was a later development. A suggestion of its inward ethical
character appears in an early formulation:

The buddhas call patience the highest penance, long-suffering the highest nibbāna; for he is not a mendicant who strikes others; he is not a monk who insults others. This is the rule of the buddhas: abstinence from sins, the institution of virtue, the inducement of a good heart.[17]

The change from the Prātimokṣa understood as an autonomous confession of faith and inward resolution, to a confession of guilt for the infraction of communal regulations may have taken place during the later phases of the Buddha's own ministry. The tradition relates that King Bimbisāra of the great state of Magadha "helped" the Buddha to institute disciplinary measures to stabilize the Saṅgha, presumably so that it might better serve the goals of the state.

Even in its disciplinary form the Prātimokṣa reflects immense respect for the autonomy of the individual monk. As he matures and begins to pursue his spiritual development independently, there is no external power to save, condemn, inhibit, or to enhance, apart from that which he cultivates himself. As he approaches the ultimate goal and experiences the certainty of enlightenment, there is in principle no charismatic power which stands over what he has gained through his own efforts, nor can any force deprive him of it.

Despite obvious formal similarities to the ideals of self-cultivation in Western monasticism and mysticism, the Buddhist yoga stands in sharp contrast with the basic conception of spiritual authority in the Christian tradition. In the medieval church the empowering grace necessary for salvation was distributed through an elaborately routinized bureaucratic hierarchy with correspondent authority—all focused in the sacrament of the Mass. The Christian monk stood under this superordinate structure. Despite many exceptions to the rule, no sector of life, monastic, clerical,

or lay, could easily escape the disciplining leverage
which could be applied at the most fundamental level,
by distributing or withholding the sacramental means of
salvation. Furthermore, on the basis of this principle,
legal-rational techniques were evolved which made it possible for the church to maintain the internal order necessary for coherent articulation with the world at large, and
to bear an unusually weighty load of mundane responsibilities in the working out of its ideals and maintaining
its standards.

The ancient Buddhist Saṅgha also possessed a highly
differentiated and rational system for the maintenance of
institutional order. But since the fundamental source of
spiritual power resided in the monk himself and was governed by his personal striving for self-perfection, no comparable system of authority could be brought against him.
It is not surprising that we find examples of the deprecation of office-based authority in the Saṅgha and its deliberate identification with the most debased motives:

The fool may desire an unreal estate, leadership among the
monks, lordship over the monasteries or honor among families:
"Let both laymen and clerics deem that this was done by me.
Let them defer to me in what ought to be done or ought not
be done." Such is the aspiration of the fool; his desires and
pride increase. One is the path toward gain, the other is the
path toward nibbāna. Understanding this well, the monk, hearer
of the Buddha, should no longer delight in worldly affairs, he
should develop life in solitude.[18]

This contrasts strikingly with the classical images of the
dignity, status, and authority of the abbot in the monastic
institutions of the West or, more radically, with the office
of the bishop in the church and his hierarchically derived
power.

With the death of the Buddha the sphere of real authority was, practically speaking, limited to the various individual monastic centers. And the mechanisms of the Vinaya which appear to be the rule of one single institution actually allow for free development of autonomous monastic units. They are not for the purpose of enforcing the unity of one monolithic church. The emphasis is always on the integrity of personal conscience. The tradition of the Council of Vaiśālī specifically reflects this general fact: the points of disagreement were held by the minority as matters of conscience, and this was the source of the "great schism," followed, the tradition says, by many other schisms.

There were also important changes in lay teaching and practice: by the end of the third century B.C., popular lay piety had begun to find its center of gravity in a cult entailing the worship of saintly relics and of the Buddha himself now raised to a supramundane plane and surrounded with symbols of his previous incarnations. This signifies the pressure of the laity for religious means increasingly remote from the monastic yoga and its goal. Even so, these cultic developments were accompanied by civilizing rationalizations of many indigenous resources which facilitated missionary activity—myths, cosmologies, gods, demons, heavens, hells, and magic—all subjected to the overarching power of the Buddha and the monastic order, and tied to educational and socializing aims. Originally the cult was simply a means for acquiring karmic merit. The early tradition asserts that "the Buddha does not desire worship, any more than an extinct fire desires fuel," but more and more the needs of the laity appear to have moved the cult in the direction of devotional theism in which the Buddha was perceived as an active living god open to prayer and supplication.[19]

With regard to the lay ethic there were significant devel-

opments. It has often been observed that both Buddhism
and Jainism showed a special affinity for the cities and for
the upwardly mobile commercial classes. This can hardly
be regarded as mere coincidence. There is an obvious relationship between the achievement standards of a developing economy and a religion where membership and status
depend on personal conversion, commitment, and individual capacity to perform. The lay ethic was rationally
oriented to the economic and political needs of the urban
mercantile and artisan classes. By contrast with the archaic
sacrificial rites, Buddhism provided less expensive religious
media. The Buddhist laity were expected to make donations to the Saṅgha, but the teaching stressed the autonomy
of the self as the sacrificial agent. More important was the
fact that the lay ethic positively reinforced economic
values. In the Theravādin text *The Admonition to Singāla*,
sometimes called the "householder's Vinaya," the layman
is exhorted to pursue a lifetime of ethical self-discipline for
the sake of well-being in "this world and the next," including the maximization of economic efficiency. He must eliminate self-indulgent and wasteful vices: sensuality, hate,
fear, and sloth. Undesirable business associates include
those who lack self-discipline and waste human and physical resources. Slave-trading (but not ownership) and other
dehumanizing practices are prohibited. The householder
must train his children in socially useful occupations and
carefully observe contractually defined ethical relationships
with his family, servants, and business associates.

This text is imbued with a "this-worldly asceticism"
which is disarmingly frank in its overt support of economic
goals:

. . . And what are the six ways of depleting wealth? They are
addiction to drink—the cause of irresponsibility; roaming the
streets at improper times; frequenting fairs; gambling; keeping

bad company; and idleness. . . . and so a man earns no new wealth but wastes what he has earned. . . .

> The wise and moral man
> Shines like a fire on a hilltop
> Making money like the bee,
> Who does not hurt the flower.
> Such a man makes his pile
> As an anthill, gradually.
> Grown wealthy, he thus
> Can help his family
> And firmly bind his friends
> To himself. He should divide
> His money in four parts;
> On one he should live,
> With two expand his trade,
> And the fourth he should save
> Against a rainy day.[20]

It is also interesting to note that the classic virtue of "noninjury" (*ahiṃsā*) is particularly important in an economy with wide-ranging spheres of commercial exchange based on contractual agreements and eschewing overt coercion—except of course through court litigation. One of the injunctions against irrational gambling (not capital investment, usury, or speculation) is based on the assertion that "a gambler's word is not respected in the law courts."

Equally important was the demand for status and fundamental human rights befitting increased economic and political power. The Buddhist theory of social stratification undercut caste criteria, not because of specific social-reforming intent, but because it denied the religious supremacy of the Brāhmans, the Vedas, and the ritual significance of caste divisions. The Buddha is represented as arguing that caste has no inherent sanctity, because it arose historically as the result of occupational differentiation, "quite naturally, and not otherwise." All men should be judged, as they once were, on the basis of their actions, not on hereditary right:

> No Brāhman is such by birth.
> No outcaste is such by birth.
> An outcaste is such by his deeds.
> A Brāhman is such by his deeds.[21]

Political theory, though basically patrimonial, asserts that the power of the state is based on a historically evolved contractual relationship between the king and the people which requires that the king earn his keep by his executive skill and moral example. In the early tradition there is no place for theories of "divine kingship."[22]

From the viewpoint of the expanding state in ancient India, Buddhism was from the very beginning a potentially valuable asset. The organized clergy, sworn to poverty, was a powerful and inexpensive medium for building solidarity where traditional collectivities had been disrupted by force, and they could assist in more subtle forms of pacifist teaching where force was impractical. This was also particularly meaningful in an expanding economy dependent on a stable and pacified environment for efficient production and exchange. The Saṅgha could provide legitimation for new political leaders who either did not have suitable ascriptive status or desired to increase their innovative power against some traditional elite.

During his long ministry the Buddha is occasionally represented in consultation with the monarchs of the various warring states, trying to make peace and inculcating rational ethical principles. The relationship between the Saṅgha and the developing state reached a climax in the third century B.C., with an event which determinatively affected the subsequent history of Buddhism. The expansion of the state of Magadha culminated in the founding

of the Mauryan empire, a patrimonially governed central
ized bureaucracy which dominated the subcontinent. The
third ruler of this empire, King Aśoka, who acceded to the
throne about 270 B.C., converted to Buddhism as a layman
after completing military consolidation of his territorial
holdings. He then issued a pacifistic ideology grounded
in part on the universal achievement-based principles common to the Buddhist ethic. This ecumenical ideology, along
with an autobiography of his own spiritual transformation
from military coercer to pious layman, was inscribed on
stones and pillars and promulgated by emissaries through
the Indian subcontinent and beyond. Its goal was to provide new values and norms for a more unified and viable
society. The traditional image of the warrior king is deliberately molded to conform with the model of inward self-
perfection and ethical discipline:

After my conquests I felt great sorrow, . . . and I began to
follow righteousness [dharma]. . . . For all beings I desire security, self-control, calm and gentleness. . . . The greatest victory
is the victory of righteousness. . . . Righteousness is having few
faults and many good deeds—mercy, charity, truthfulness and
purity. . . . The goal is to escape from evil inclinations . . .
cruelty, harshness, anger, pride, envy, idleness, obstinacy, bad
temper. . . .[23]

His publicized transformation and its values have an
ascetic quality drawn from the resources of the major
salvation religions. Many Buddhist sayings convey the
same idea:

Compared with the man who conquers thousands in battle, the
greatest warrior is the man who conquers himself. . . . If a man
is strenuous, thoughtful, self-controlled, and morally disciplined,
he grows immensely.[24]

Aśoka's ideology exhorts all men in the empire to
cooperative pursuit of socially and economically efficient

virtues. It discourages the practice of archaic sacrificial
and magical ceremonials, thus undercutting traditional religious customs that reinforced politically troublesome local
groups and supported an entrenched class of archaic religious practitioners. The ideology makes no specific mention
of Brāhmanic caste criteria for social integration, urging
only that Brāhmans be shown the same respect as other
religious leaders.

Show good behavior towards slaves and servants, obedience to
mother and father, generosity towards friends, acquaintances,
and relatives and towards ascetics and Brāhmans, and abstention
from killing living beings.[25]

There is no way to establish the specific legal reforms,
if any, which he undertook to implement these views.
What is certain, however, is that the inscriptions do not
formally endorse caste laws, as do the inscriptions of later
Hindu monarchs.

Although Aśoka did not institute Buddhism as the state
religion, he promoted Buddhist missionary movements,
which spilled over the borders into other lands—most
importantly into Ceylon.[26] Several of his edicts indicate
that he tried to unify the Saṅgha and stem sectarian conflicts which threatened effective support of the state. He
may have instituted a doctrinal reform by convening a
third council at the capital city of Pāṭaliputra, which then
became the basis for later Therāvadin orthodoxy. But
schismatic movements persisted for the doctrinal and institutional reasons noted above. The ancient Saṅgha appears to have been an inherently unstable platform on
which to ground a worldly ideology no matter how benign.

Within fifty years after Aśoka's death the Mauryan empire collapsed under a multitude of pressures: barbarian
invasions, economic decline, internal political conflict, and

a resurgence of Brāhmanic power. Subsequently, the ascriptive principles of the caste system were further rationalized. The king's responsibility was increasingly tied to the maintenance of the social order in accordance with Brāhmanic values, thus forming the permanent social base for the emergence of normative Hinduism. In 185 B.C. the Mauryan dynasty was replaced by a new elite, the Śungas, whose founder assassinated the last Mauryan ruler and declared himself king, appropriating Vedic ceremonial and prerogatives. Buddhist teaching remained influential in some of the Śunga feudatories, but its social theory was slowly pushed into a peripheral position—allowing for occasional legitimation of invading "barbarian" kings and their courts—chiefly among Greeks, Sakas, Pahlavas, and Kuṣāṇas. Several of these monarchs, most notably the Indo-Greek King Menandros (*ca.* 160-140 B.C.), and the Kuṣāṇa King Kaniṣka (A.D. 78-103) who ruled over a short-lived empire in northern India, were vigorous supporters of the religion and contributed significantly to the growth of Buddhist culture and art.[27] However, by far the most important events during this period surround the development of Mahāyāna.

Mahāyāna Buddhism did not emerge identifiably as a self-conscious movement with its own distinctive literature and institutions until the first century A.D. Its earliest sūtras —held to contain the true and restored teachings of the Buddha—cannot be dated with certainty before the beginnings of the Christian era, and there is some indication of Western and Iranian influence on their doctrine and symbolism. The problem is complicated by the lack of historical data for the specific points of origin and social grounding of these materials. However, many prominent Mahāyāna principles have their roots in the issues raised at the second Council of Vaiśālī, which culminated in the schism of the Mahāsaṅghika school.[28] Its doctrines and those developed by other forerunners of the Mahāyāna represented liberalizing solutions to cumulative tensions which had been present within the Saṅgha almost from the beginning. Particularly controversial were the hardened dichotomy between the laity and the monastic elite, and disagreements regarding the right of lay access to the full religious goal.

The issues at stake centered on the traditional conception of monastic perfection, ideally embodied in the *arhat* ("worthy one," saint), the fully perfected monk who attains complete enlightenment only at the end of the long and arduous process of self-discipline demanded by the yoga. This and related ideals were held by the liberals to be "selfish" distortions of the original teaching, not only violating the model of the Buddha's compassion for all men, but subtly reinforcing the taint of self-seeking and craving. The failures of the early Hīnayāna schools, though often exaggerated in Mahāyāna polemics, nevertheless are subtly reflected in some of the Hīnayāna traditions: most notably in the idea that there had been an early period of pristine spiritual power in the life of the community when many monks had attained enlightenment with ease. But as time went on there were fewer men who had the necessary talents—a view based on the old theory of historical degeneration—that the Buddha's teaching must slowly lose its vitality as men became more depraved and less capable of perceiving the eternal truths of the Dharma.

This reflects the endemic problems inherent in the doctrine and the process of institutionalization: the teaching was increasingly compounded with scholastic accretions which—though they aimed to clarify—also routinized the practice in detail, particularly as it was dispersed among a number of schools each with its own polemics and

dogma. And there were many frustrations attendant on
the struggle for self-perfection in a framework increasingly
remote in time from the charisma of the historical Buddha.
The lengthy and methodical structure of the yoga promoted the polarization of nirvāṇa as an "otherworldly"
and distant spiritual reward, which in turn further exacerbated the elaboration of yogic striving. The commentaries
and treatises of the various Hīnayāna schools are massive
encyclopedias which bear witness to these scholastic developments.

In addition, the worldly possessions and commitments
of the Saṅgha raised a central doctrinal problem considerably more important than the issues surrounding monastic poverty and ascetic rigor: this was the paradoxical
conflict between the obligations of the monk to pursue
his own salvation "alone, like the rhinoceros" and to serve
other sentient creatures with compassion and specific acts
of worldly service. Monastic withdrawal and isolation had
the ironic potential of reinforcing a compulsive sense of
"self-power" or, conversely, of hopelessness—each of which
could be massively dysfunctional for certain types of personalities. Related to this was the question of moral and
psychic perfection: one of the earliest accusations directed
against the arhat was that he could be the victim of erotic
fantasies, dreams, and other imperfections reflecting spiritual regression.

In an effort to resolve these problems, the forerunners
of Mahāyāna appropriated an old sacred archetype of the
early tradition and transformed it into a new model of
spiritual perfection. This was the ideal of the *bodhisattva*
("one whose essence is enlightenment" or, freely, "essential
Buddha"). The term was originally used chiefly to denote
previous incarnations of the historical Buddha. In its new
form it was universalized. It means one who, although

worthy of nirvāṇa, sacrifices this ultimate satisfaction in order to help all sentient creatures with acts of love and compassion as the precondition of his own salvation. All men are inherently capable of filling this role. It is not necessarily a monastic category.[29]

This significantly undercut the rigidities of the class distinction between monk and layman. Although monasticism continued as a central institution, the bodhisattva ideal opened the teaching to new symbolic forms, beliefs, and practices. It facilitated popular diffusion and provided the basis for theistic and philosophical developments reflected in the principal Mahāyāna texts and schools. Equally important was the overt affirmation of the divinity of the Buddha. He is not only the historical teacher; he is an omnipresent deity, an eternal spiritual being and active force. This allowed for the development of a theory of continued revelation with innovative doctrinal and institutional consequences.

The *Perfection of Wisdom Sūtras* are among the most important theoretical formulations of Mahāyāna teaching. The bodhisattva's distinctive marks are loving compassion and wisdom. This wisdom and its perfection are related not only to self-sacrificing love but also to a more accurate understanding of the nature of nirvāṇa. It is not an otherworldly goal in polarity with the phenomenal world. This is a distortion which ironically reduces it to a spatio-temporal object and reinforces the craving inimical to salvation. Nirvāṇa is beyond all phenomenal and conceptual polarities—void and empty (*śūnya*). As one approaches inward realization of this truth and experiences enlightened insight, all distinctions between nirvāṇa and the world are obliterated. The bodhisattva lives in pure, egoless compassion. And the phenomenal world itself is thus sanctified by the liberating intuition of the illusoriness of the cognitive distinction between nirvāṇa and saṃsāra.

At the level of everyday cognition there is a logical con-
tradiction in the notion that nirvāṇa and saṃsāra are not
different, but "void"; and that a relationship of love must
be cultivated with phenomena—discrete "persons"—which
are illusory. But these antinomies are not only amenable
to, but actually enhance the value of, mystical insight.
The bodhisattva's heroic spiritual prowess lies in his ability
to transcend and incorporate these contradictions. And
once he has achieved this, it is the source of his power
to save himself and others.

Moreover, this ideal reinforced the value of action in
the world and the redemptive value of suffering, both of
which were important in providing the basis for a missionary ideology with the necessary strength to brave the
hazards and hostilities of the everyday world:

> The bodhisattva is lonely, without a companion. He puts on
> the armor of supreme wisdom. He acts by himself, and leaves
> nothing to others, working with a steel will of courage and
> strength. . . . He resolves that "the virtue of generosity is not
> my helper—I am the helper of generosity. The virtues of moral-
> ity, patience, courage, meditation, and wisdom do not help me;
> it is I who sustain them. . . . All karmic pain and evil I take
> on my own body. . . . I must bear the burden of all beings . . .
> to save them all."[30]

It is important to note that these Mahāyāna innovations
represent the deliberate selection and systematization of
ideas already present in the earlier traditions; and the
Mahāyāna sūtras themselves, although relatively late, are
the product of developments which had long since been
underway. The special configuration of early Mahāyāna
symbolism is an organic part of the missionary growth of
the community, though it is presented as a purified form
of the essential teachings.

Philosophical refinements based on the śūnya motif in the *Wisdom Sūtras* were developed by the philosopher Nāgārjuna (*ca.* A.D. 200), founder of the Mādhyamika ("middle position school"), and one of the most powerful intellects in Indian history. He evolved a negational logic designed to break the inveterate tendency of the finite human mind to impose spatio-temporal categories on the supreme spiritual goal. The rigor of the teaching attributed to him often appears nihilistic, since its aim is primarily to refute all metaphysical systems; but it also positively guards the concept of nirvāṇa and related values against reduction to an entity in polarity with the phenomenal world.[31] This doctrine or, rather, critical razor was not developed to support one form of predication or theory against another, but, rather, to undercut all dogmas and varieties of dualistic cognition. The "middle way" equates the law of "dependent origination" with the insight that all phenomena are illusory consequences of subject-object predication—including especially the debilitating opposition of "being and nonbeing" both of which are subtle ontologies, since the one evokes the other. The desire for annihilation is the same as the desire for "being" itself. Profound understanding of this leads to a salient religious awakening and a direct intuition of the highest truth.

The potential antinomian consequences of the assertion that everyday human experiences and institutions are empty of inherent value was met by a doctrine of relative or pragmatic truth: men must live from day to day predominantly in a real (if ultimately illusory) world governed by karmic laws important in practical affairs, demanding rigorous ethical standards. Moral perfection is a ladder which is provisionally necessary to reach higher mystical insight. The stages of moral perfection and the yoga itself, are likened to a raft constructed to cross the river of saṃsāra which may be abandoned only after reaching the other shore.

The other major philosophical school, the Vijñānavāda ("consciousness doctrine")—also called Yogācāra ("Yoga-way")—based its teachings on sūtras developed around idealistic conceptions: all objective perceptions are illusory projections of the mind ("the mind, like a skillful painter, creates the various and sundry aggregates"). Salvation is achieved by exhausting the source of dualistic consciousness and sensory perception through a yoga which leads to union with the pure, primordial ground of consciousness itself. The teaching has ontological connotations, since it seems to affirm a fixed source for all phenomena, though it is also asserted that the perfected mind no longer projects its own external world, and only perceives the phenomenal world as it is projected by the minds of the ignorant.

This radical subjective idealism made it difficult to provide a solid rationale for ethics, since no real relationship exists between the perfected self and the objective world: The general problem is stated in the question: "How, in the absence of an object, can bodhisattvas . . . be born at will for the service of all things?"[32] The answer given is that "the personality which a bodhisattva assumes is not real, and yet it is perceived when he works for the benefit of all beings." The problem of validating the bodhisattva's obligation to act in this illusory charade is answered, once again, by tying the fate of the individual to the fate of all other creatures; and this link is reinforced by the fact that the primary symbols are loaded in favor of a theory of permanent being: "pure consciousness" (*vijñaptimātratā*); essential "suchness" (*tathatā*); "store consciousness" (*ālayavijñāna*); "womb of the Buddha" (*Tathāgatagarbha*);[33] "own being" (*svabhāvika*). The radical illusionist theorem tended to give way to the idea of an immutable reality

behind phenomena. This metaphysical predisposition gave
the bodhisattva and related moral norms a pragmatic ontological status which was reinforced in the everyday framework of cultic worship and ethical discipline.

In exploring these antinomies the philosophical schools
reached extraordinary heights of exaltation and subtlety.
They liberated the mystical ideal from conservative scholasticism, attracted many intellectuals, and provided new
principles for development of Mahāyāna universalism.

Missionary diffusion was facilitated by a remarkable
principle of rationalization which allowed for almost unlimited adaptability to given conditions. This was the idea
of the Buddha's "skill-in-means" (*upāyakauśalya*)—the
ability to adjust teachings and institutions to the needs of
all sorts and conditions of men. It was identified with the
Buddha's universal love, and, combined with the paradoxical conviction that all phenomenal forms are illusory
and void, it allowed for expedient use of new techniques
to further the message of salvation. It cut through traditional boundaries, textual literalism, and orthodox formulations with remarkable power and carried the teaching
forward.

The bulk of Mahāyāna practice found its popular social
base through theistic means. The heavens were filled with
saving buddhas and bodhisattvas, who transferred their
own merit to the believer in response to prayer, provided
richly differentiated objects for cultic worship, and satis-
fied a wide range of personal needs. Devotional piety had
earlier inspired important artistic achievements, beginning
with King Aśoka in the third century B.C., and in the
monuments at Bhārhut and Sāñcī, later culminating in the
superb Buddha statuary of the Mathurā and Gandhāra
schools—the latter clearly influenced by Greco-Roman art
forms.[34]

Among many efforts to systematize this theistic profusion, the most important was the formulation of the *Trikāya* ("three bodies") Buddhology. Here the Buddha exists as an eternal spiritual essence, as a supreme heavenly deity, and in worldly manifestations. He is both the ground of being and the actional agent of salvation. He interpenetrates all discrete phenomena, assuring the universal presence of the Buddha-nature among all creatures, without distinction. This theory provided a dynamic metaphysic which could be adjusted to new social and cultural circumstances. And since the universe is infused with the divine essence, no aspect of the world is without transforming potential; it is inherently a sanctified ground: "The Body of the perfect Buddha irradiates everything, its essential 'suchness' (tathatā) is undifferentiated, and the road to Buddhahood is open to all. . . ."[35]

The structural similarity of the Trikāya doctrine to the Christian Trinitarian formula is of course marked, though there are important differences, one of the most significant being the assertion that all worldly manifestations of the Buddha are both illusory and manifold. However, what is most striking about the doctrine in contrast with the earlier teaching of universal flux and impermanence is its approximation to a theory of absolute being with an internal dialectic:

The Three Bodies are one and the same for all the Buddhas for three reasons: 1) *basis*, for the absolute basis of phenomena (*dharmadhātu*) is indivisible; 2) *tendency*, because there is no tendency particular to one Buddha and not to another; and 3) *act*, because their actions are common to all. And the Three Bodies have a threefold stability: 1) *nature*, for the Body of Essence (*Dharmakāya*) is essentially stable; 2) *persistence*, for the Body of Bliss (*Sambhogakāya*) experiences phenomena unceasingly; and 3) *connection*, for the Created Body (*Nirmāṇa-*

kāya), once it has passed away, shows its metamorphoses again and again.[36]

Within the immensely rich theistic literature are several important sūtras which became the basis of the most popular cults and schools in China and Japan. The *Lotus of the Good Law* purports to reveal the ultimate teaching of the Buddha, now the transcendent father of all worlds, whose love bridges all finite limitations. The devotee is saved by faith in this sūtra itself. There is a suggestion of sectarian exclusiveness in the dogma that it embodies the only efficacious means of salvation, which exhausts all other doctrines. It opens the door to all forms of devotional piety:

I have made a vow to cause all creatures to rank equally with me. . . . Even children who, in play, gathered sand for a Buddha's stupa, . . . and those who by offering a single flower . . . a small sound . . . folding the hands . . . a slight gesture. . . . They will attain the perfect nirvāna.[37]

The sūtra also contains a chapter devoted to magical incantations; and in general it reflects an immense concern for unlimited lay participation.

More radical are the *Land of Bliss Sūtras*. Here Amitābha ("unlimited light") Buddha presides over a heavenly paradise—the "pure land"—available to the faithful through the power of his grace. Eschatological motifs appear, stressing the uselessness of all techniques of self-salvation in a world of utter degeneracy and emphasizing the need to rely devotedly on Amitābha's love. In this framework the last vestige of yogic "self-power," the quandaries of the anattā doctrine, and even the immutable law of karma were resolutely placed under the Buddha's compassionate authority.

Though Mahāyāna produced little in the way of sys-

tematic economic or political theory, there are some
exceptions which deserve mention because of their de-
monstrable influence in China and Japan. The *Exposition
of Vimalakīrti* glorifies the virtues of a paradigmatic layman and bodhisattva who not only pursue a life of rational
economic gain and sophisticated worldly well-being but
achieves a spiritual perfection excelling that of the most
distinguished monks. His accomplishments are somewhat
paradoxical but clearly in accord with the bodhisattva
model:

... Though but a simple layman, yet observing pure monastic
     discipline.
Living at home, yet never desirous of anything;
Possessing wife and children, yet always exercising pure virtues;
Surrounded by his family, yet aloof from worldly pleasures;
Bedecked with jeweled ornaments, yet adorned with spiritual
     splendor;
Eating and drinking, yet enjoying the flavor of meditation;
Frequenting the gambling house, yet leading the gamblers into
     the right path;
In the house of debauchery, yet manifesting to all the error of
     passion ...
Profiting by all professions, yet far above being absorbed by
     them.[38]

In the area of political theory the *Excellent Golden
Light Sūtra* outlines a modified doctrine of divine kingship.
The king is a *devaputra* ("son of the gods"), a designation
also current in the Hindu theory of kingship, but he has
no insulated cultic status. He stands under the Buddha's
law and is obliged to promote universal peace and social
order or by judgment of the gods forgo his right to rule.
"When the king is negligent the gods say: 'This king is
unrighteous ...' and from the wrath of the gods his kingdom will perish." This is mixed with a utopian model of
universal peace which is genuinely redolent of the massive

problems of economic and social order throughout Indian history:

When the eighty-four thousand kings of India are content with their own territories . . . they will not attack one another or raise mutual strife. . . . And all living beings in India will be rich with all kinds of goods and corn, very prosperous but not greedy.[39]

The patrimonial theory of kingship remained dominantly contractual, but problems of social stratification receive only passing attention, and caste is presupposed as an institutional reality. One looks in vain for a critique comparable to that found in some of the scriptures of the early tradition.

Brāhmanic social and political theory was decisively institutionalized during the Gupta empire (320-540), and the diffusion of Brāhmanic values was vastly extended within the wide sphere of Gupta imperial authority. The detailed travelogues of several Chinese Buddhist pilgrims to India show that the Gupta rulers, though Hindus, supported Buddhist art, philosophy, and devotionalism. But the literary and epigraphic materials also show that they systematically reinforced caste and divine-kingship institutions, certainly the only effective means for maintaining social order given the immense heterogeneity and endemic problems of conflict in the subcontinent. The devastating invasions of the White Huns in the mid-fifth century exacerbated these problems, and finally precipitated the collapse of the empire.

However, in this situation of profound disturbance Buddhism underwent an extraordinary metamorphosis. Beginning recognizably in the sixth and seventh centuries A.D. there was an upsurge of a vast new repertoire of magical, ritualistic, and erotic symbolism, which formed the basis of Tantric Buddhism. The term is of uncertain etymology (perhaps from the root *tan*, "extend," "continue," "develop"). Its distinguishing institutional characteristic was the communication through an intimate master-disciple relationship of doctrines and practices contained in the secret Buddhist Tantric texts and held to be the Buddha's most potent teachings, reserved for the initiate alone. Significantly, this esoteric institution was considerably less vulnerable to the vicissitudes of the times than its exoteric monastic counterpart precisely because of its anonymity and secrecy.

In content, Tantric Buddhism is fused in many areas almost indistinguishably with Mahāyāna doctrines and archaic and magical Hinduism. Cryptic obscurities were deliberately imposed on the texts to make them inscrutable except to the gnostic elite. But it took a number of identifiable forms, the most dramatic of which was Vajrayāna ("thunderbolt vehicle"). Vajrayāna had its metaphysical roots in the supposition that the dynamic spiritual and natural powers of the universe are driven by interaction between male and female elements, of which man himself is a microcosm. Its mythological base was in a pantheon of paired deities, male and female, whose sacred potency, already latent in the human body, was evoked through an actional yoga of ritualistic meditations on visual iconographs (*maṇḍala*), magical formulae (*mantra*), symbolic gestures (*mudrā*) and—most strikingly—through sexual intercourse, which occasionally included radical antinomian behavior. The inward vitality of the sacred life-force is realized most powerfully in sexual union, because there nonduality is experienced in full psychophysical perfection.

This doctrine seems to invert almost every feature of the early tradition, but it is nevertheless imbued with a deep inner logic. Its philosophical justification was derived from adaptations of Yogācāra and Mādhyamika theory;

since the phenomenal world is fundamentally identical with the spiritual universe of "emptiness" or is at most an illusory projection of the mind, the conclusion was drawn that all moral distinctions are not only devoid of real content, but may serve as expedient "means" (*upāya*) to a substantive spiritual end: the overcoming of the illusory sense of duality between the phenomenal and spiritual worlds. For the adept it is not only necessary to say that there is no good or evil; it must be proved in an active way. Consequently, violation of traditional morality actually speeds the realization of nonduality.

The *Hevajra Tantra*—one of the most influential texts —states that "those who have 'means' (*upāya*) are liberated ... through the very thing by which wicked people are bound. The world is bound by lust, and released by the same lust."[40] The decisive focus of this practice is on the existential realization (*sādhana*) and positive experience of liberation through the instrument of the physical body. Nirvāṇa, though "void" and beyond conceptualization, nevertheless can and must be experienced as ultimate bliss (*mahāsukha*) engendered through available physical resources, the most salient being human sexuality. This does not represent a debasement of religious values as much as it represents a sanctification of sexuality—an idea of great antiquity both in India and in other ancient cultures. In keeping with the somatic and physiological focus of this teaching we find the affirmation of a positive and vital ontology: the term *vajra* also means "diamond," signifying an adamantine purity and lasting substance which is the essential nature of the realization of "voidness": "*Śūnyatā* which is firm, substantial, indivisible, and impenetrable, proof against fire and imperishable, is called *vajra.*"

An underlying current in this and comparable formula-

tions is the search for bodily perfection leading to immortality—"health" in the ultimate and worldly sense. The
yoga was based in part on an ancient mystical physiology
in which the latent spiritual resources of the body were
activated sequentially in feeling states developing through
the interior hierarchy of neural centers with sacred and
health-giving properties. This inner physiology of the body
is often regarded as a hierophony in its own right. Saraha
—the great poet and master of the Sahajayāna ("innate
vehicle") school—exalts the inherent spiritual powers of
the human body:

Here [within the body] is the Ganges and the Jumnā [rivers];
. . . here are [the holy cities of] Prayāga and Benares. Here
the sun and moon. . . . I have not seen a place of pilgrimage
and an abode of bliss like my body.[41]

And elsewhere we also find the flat assertion that "he who
has studied Sahaja becomes at once perfect; no more will
he suffer from disease and death."

Though classical asceticism was swept away, these practices were placed under strict ritual controls. The adept
and his consort ("young, beautiful, and intelligent") were
required to meditate at length on the purified spiritual
meaning of the erotic act both before and during intercourse. Sexuality in any other form is animalistic and positively degrading. Consequently, the ideal model is one of
sacramental sanctification and transfiguration.

Paralytic anxieties associated with the stifling of sexual
impulses are alleviated by the controlled "acting out" of
these desires. We find ritual intercourse prescribed for
certain types of personalities, perhaps only once, to break
the bondage of fear—the negative "attachment" to the
illusory seductiveness of life. Even in its positive and
aggressive form this enterprise often ambiguously values

sexuality as a means for mystical liberation, because it
affirms the necessity of breaking through artificial moral
barriers for the final purpose of purging sexual desire.

The Tantric master Āryadeva (*ca.* 650) says:

> Discrimination is the demon who
> Produces the ocean of transmigration. . . .
> So, with all one's might, one should do
> Whatever fools condemn.
> And with a pure mind
> Dwell in union with one's divinity [sexual consort].
> The mystics, pure in mind,
> Dally with lovely girls,
> Infatuated with the poisonous flame of passion,
> That they may be set free from desire. . . .[42]

Ideally, the passions should be purified and transformed,
never acted out on whim; but this rationale could lead
to abuses. The indirect legitimation of amoral extremes is
present in some of the Tantras: "Perfection can be had
by satisfying all one's desires," not excluding incest, can-
nibalism, adultery, lying, stealing, and killing.[43] This consequence of the conviction that moral norms are illusory
impediments to enlightenment was on the whole held in
check by everyday institutional pressures and by occasional
assertions that these extremes are practiced only by the
"lower castes." But caste itself was subject to a unique
criticism: In the state of nonduality all worldly forms and
institutions are the same—"there is neither Śūdra nor
Brāhman"; and one of the most efficacious blows at social and ethical conventions is the deliberate selection
of an outcaste woman as a consort, through whom all
routine moral and aesthetic barriers may be broken most
potently.[44]

These rites, however, were not the common practice.[45]
The exalted liturgy of Tantric meditation and ritual is in

fact an extraordinarily viable art form: the maṇḍalas represent a system of coded iconography capable of many variations but always depicting a sacred cosmology and theophany which the yogin internalizes through fixed meditation, prepared first by rites of initiation into their secrets. The body and its psychic forces are transformed into an integrated microcosm of the spiritual powers embedded in the maṇḍala which penetrates the universe. Direct ontological participation in the sublime world of the omnipresent buddhas and bodhisattvas purifies the self, expunges fear, desire, guilt, and the power of death. The incorporation of these sacred values may be simultaneously enhanced and expressed outwardly through the mudrās —physical reflexes of cathected inner truths. Equally important is the mantra, a short, frequently coded, prayer or formula which distills the meaning of essential teachings. Key texts were often summed up and expressed in a single syllable or short phrase held to possess magical efficacy. The idea of the magical power of the spoken word was embedded deeply in the archaic Vedic liturgies and traditional magic. In the Tantric setting the mantra technique evolved into an independent school—the Mantrayāna ("true-word vehicle"), which was influential in China and Japan: "What is there that cannot be accomplished by mantras if they are applied in accordance with the rules?" The "rules," of course, are crucial—beginning first with submission to the authority of the guru—and developed within the liturgical discipline and social controls of the cult.[46]

The *Kālacakra* ("wheel of time") *Tantra* stresses the special relevance of Tantric practices in an eschatological setting: the present "dark age" (*kāliyuga*) of historical and moral decline requires the use of many expedient techniques—including mystical astrology and the sexual yoga—which will allow escape from the domination of time and decay.[47] It presents the Buddha as a kind of creator god who controls the forces of time and mortality; and the creator motif appears even more directly in the related concept of the "primal Buddha" (*Ādibuddha*) from whom all other sacred forms have evolved. Tantric Buddhology also appropriated a theistic solar mythology already present in Mahāyāna: in the *Mahāvairocana Tantra*, the Buddha Vairocana ("irradiant," "shining out") is elevated to celestial status as the principal member of the specifically Tantric pantheon. This was richly developed for meditational and devotional purposes, predominating in the symbolism of many maṇḍalas and rites.

Tantrism also absorbed a host of primitive shamanistic practices and techniques of black magic with wide-ranging popular appeal, including a pantheon of demons and "wrathful" divinities who could act variously as guardians for the highest teachings or empower spells for the aversion of evil and attainment of specific worldly goals. The Indo-Tibetan form of Buddhist Tantrism was deeply immersed in these archaic techniques, incorporated where appropriate under the higher values of cultured Mahāyāna and Tantric teachings. In general, Buddhist Tantrism assimilated and synthesized a vast range of loosely related elements from the substratum of indigenous Indian spirituality—gross and fine—most of which it transformed into useful pedagogical and cultic tools.

It is not surprising that we look in vain for specifically social-reforming or systematic political formulations. The Indian Tantric cults—as secret "voluntary associations"—were in this respect true to the main thrust of the great tradition: all religious means were channeled to support techniques of personal salvation, not for the purpose of altering given socio-economic and political institutions.

However, we must exercise care in interpreting this fact; the social origins and class stratification of Tantric Buddhism are almost impossible to determine. Tantric Hinduism, also, was in vogue during this period; and its popularity suggests that a wide-ranging culture of religious and magical esotericism had broken through stereotyped pressures resulting from the imposition of state-controlled Brāhmanic institutions during the Gupta era. In this we can detect the irregular but very real outlines of a protest against elite "orthodox" hierarchies and dogmas, and the search for freedom and catharsis through media intimately suited to personal religious needs. In addition, Tantrism gained specific institutional support from the patronage of the independent Pāla dynasty (750-1150) in Bengal; and many of the Bengali poets show the inspiration of Tantric values—the exaltation and spiritual valorization of the self and the natural world, openly opposed to Brāhmanic orthodoxy.[48] The Pāla kings helped to establish the great Buddhist university of Vikramaśīla, which was a major center of traditional as well as of Tantric Buddhism. Long-lasting commercial contacts with Indonesia brought Buddhist values within the sphere of Southeast Asian culture—particularly in Java and Sumatra.

However, after the ninth century A.D. Indian Buddhism began a perceptible decline, for reasons which are still far from clear.[49] The Mahāyāna philosophical schools became increasingly preoccupied with abstruse theoretical issues centered around problems of logic, epistemology, and perception. In time theistic Mahāyāna and Tantric Buddhism became hardly distinguishable from the increasingly luxuriant garden of Hinduism. The great medieval Hindu philosopher Śaṅkara (788-820) successfully incorporated major features of Buddhist philosophy in a decisive Brāhmanic synthesis. Buddhist monasteries, schools, and cults began to lose their popular social grounding, and we can see the slow but sure absorption of its symbolism, intellectual leadership, and laity into the richness of the increasingly dominant Hindu culture. The Buddha was represented as one among many incarnations of the Hindu god Viṣṇu. The final blow came with the Turko-Muslim invasions in the twelfth century. Offended by monasticism in principle, shocked by polytheistic Mahāyāna and Tantrism, and coveting the wealth of the monasteries, the invaders systematically extirpated Buddhism by force. It was not to return as a significant institutional reality for eight hundred years, though its traces remained in folk cults and many adumbrated forms, particularly in Kashmir, Orissa, and Bengal.

2. China

THE DECISIVE FACTOR affecting the history of Buddhism in China was its confrontation with the religious values and institutions of a high civilization which differed markedly from the dominantly ascetic, otherworldly orientation of Indian Buddhism. The Buddhist world-view made its own unique contributions to Chinese culture, while at the same time undergoing reciprocal acculturation which produced a new if not always stable synthesis of Indian and Chinese values.

In China during the first century A.D., Buddhism was confined mainly to foreign communities in the northern commercial cities. The Buddha was worshiped popularly as one among many deities imbued with magical powers and considered worthy of petition and propitiation; but it was not until the arrival of Mahāyāna missionaries and texts from Central Asia that systematic propagation was undertaken. Its deeper values and institutions began to assume relatively clear definition and to find social grounding among members of the gentry class.[1]

Penetration was hastened by the severe political and

economic disorders which occurred at the end of the later
Han dynasty (A.D. 25-220). In A.D. 184, the empire was
torn by a series of massive revolts followed by violent
repression and warlordism, and in this situation of general social breakdown Buddhism provided more potent
answers to pressing questions about the meaning of the
times and of life itself not manageable within the indigenous religious framework. Han Confucianism formed the
basis for a highly rational political system, and its ethic
had immense integrative strength. However, its cosmo-
logical metaphysic was designed to reinforce worldly
institutions, obligations, and goals. Awareness of the
meaning of the self and the world, and of the ambiguities
of life was sometimes profound, as with Mencius and his
disciples; but self-reflection and inward cultivation were
aimed at better performance of the *li*—proper social action,
not personal salvation.

Taoism, with its naturalistic mysticism, provided an
important outlet for the socially induced tensions and the
pressures of conventional civilization. Related to it was
the "mysterious learning" (*hsüen-hsüeh*), an esoteric gnosis
with a comparatively sophisticated metaphysic in which
problems of ontology, the hidden ground of worldly order,
of being and nonbeing were of concern. Both mystical
Taoism and hsüen-hsüeh were symptomatic of a deep-felt
need for personal transcendence beyond the givenness of
life and world-affirming cosmologies. But hsüen-hsüeh
appears as a metaphysical capstone to Confucianism, subtly
reinforcing traditional values by augmenting its intellectual prestige with speculative and mystical motifs. And
cultic Taoism was dominantly shamanistic, providing
magical techniques for immortality in this world, not
the next.[2]

Buddhism was something very different. It was not a

philosophical theory providing an intellectually satisfying
explanation of the universe. Nor was it a mystical gnosis
stressing the spirituality of the natural world. It was a
way of life and regularized behavior aiming at personal
salvation, demanding total commitment and centered on
a new institution—the monastery—a tightly knit solidarity,
resilient, disciplined, and intent on its own unique goals.
The autonomy of the monastic order was based on an
endemic—if at first only dimly perceived—set of values
exemplified by the monk and his calling. This in turn provided a new space-time continuum not only for the freeing
of thought and traditional forms, but for the spiritual
reconstruction of life itself, paradoxically leading the individual away from the everyday world to final emancipation from the fetters of birth and death. With its
devaluation of phenomenal life and rich repertoire of otherworldly symbolism, it placed infinite worth on the legitimacy of personal striving for salvation at the cost of all
worldly concerns. By comparison, the indigenous religions
and philosophies were life-affirming and naturalistic.

It is true that Buddhism was often far from being adequately understood. The Sanskrit texts could only with
great difficulty be translated into the Chinese. Key concepts like nirvāṇa and śūnya were translated with the
Taoist *wu-wei* which connotes a this-worldly "nonactivity"
—an absence of anxiety and striving—rather than an absolute condition of transcendence and the annihilation of
all spatio-temporal categories. Even so, the perception
of Buddhist values was first mediated by the indigenous
mystical tradition, and the Buddhist world-view slowly cut
through this opaque surface.

Most important was the model of the celibate monk
and the institutionally defined goals of the monastic order.
The Buddhist monastery, however worldly it may often

have become, served as the setting for full-time pursuit of the otherworldly goal. Despite important similarities, the Buddhist monk could not be mistaken for the Taoist recluse—the "retired gentleman." Even more striking was the stark contrast between the monk and the ideal Confucian "gentleman"—the *chün-tzu*—with his rigorous commitment to the principles of worldly solidarity, filial piety, and loyalty to the state.

It is not surprising that the decisive and ultimately victorious opponents of Buddhism in China were the Confucian literati. Their categorical affirmation of the inherent value of the phenomenal world, of the need for clearly structured human obligations and rational social order, was deeply violated by the ideal of the ascetic monk abandoning the world, his family, and the principle of filial piety for the sake of an unknown, incomprehensible reward. The monastic ideal was regarded by many Confucians as an immense threat to the family, state, and every sacred value.

As Buddhism gained popular support among the gentry and began to penetrate lower social levels through the appropriation of indigenous cultic and magical means, both Confucian and Taoist leaders tried to block its advance. And for the next millennium—until the final victory of Neo-Confucianism in the Sung dynasty, Buddhist and Confucian divines engaged in sharp polemics and power struggles centering around their radically different views of the meaning and conduct of life. At a less articulate level, Buddhist and Taoist leaders vied with each other for pre-eminence in popular magic and favor at the royal court. Buddhist theorists sought to minimize the accusations flung at the ascetic teaching by systematically incorporating the Confucian ethic and requiring that the laity give it full support. The "five relationships" were often fused with the law of karmic retribution and the five precepts, and the laity were urged to obey the law of the land; but the conflict remained basically insoluble. This was not so much because synthetic accommodations were inherently uncongenial—Mahāyāna had a long tradition of assimilative expertise. Rather, the basic conflict was in the socially grounded hostility between the Buddhist and the Confucian elites with respect to their most fundamental values.

At first Buddhism found its devotees mainly from among the mercantile and urban gentry. They were not a homogenous group; the bulk were petty merchants and landowners far removed from the aristocracy and great feudal families. What they had in common for the most part was a rudimentary literary education in the classics which could qualify them for lower-echelon positions in the magistracy. The majority seem to have been of "lowly origin" in the sense that they came from gentry families that had fallen on hard times as China slid into chaos during the later Han. The Saṅgha was in principle not only free from class discrimination but provided a new cultural center and a new form of achievement attractive to talented men of religious sensibilities who were largely barred from their traditional pursuits. Most of the old avenues of success were closed, and even where the opportunity for bureaucratic advancement existed, it had a hollow ring; the public life was full of hazard. In addition, the monasteries became centers of eclectic study. Taoists discovered a more effective road to immortality in the meditation techniques of the yoga, and in the elaborated doctrine of the "void," and they brought their own traditions with them.

One index of the widely varied motives behind gentry conversions in Han times lies in the evidence of an antinomian "underground" culture with an interest in ritual affirmation of the condition of chaos for its own sake, an undirected and aimless freedom from the artificial restraints and moribund values of the times. There were Buddho-Taoist adepts whose fame lay in their bizarre and unconventional life-style: wine, drugs, sex—anything to provoke the experience of release and escape the meshes of the dying routine.[3] Equally important were the inherent tensions in the classical Chinese family system: in the context of familial hierarchies and patrimonialism, the principle of "filial piety" could be a form of excruciating bondage in which deep hostilities evoked a longing for social and spiritual freedom.

In the second and third centuries important Buddhist centers were located at two great commercial cities: at the capital Lo-yang and at P'eng-ch'eng. At Lo-yang the Chinese devotees translated a number of Mahāyāna sūtras, including versions of the *Perfection of Wisdom* and *Pure Land* materials. We catch a glimpse of the integrity of the Lo-yang church from the fact that its members addressed each other as "bodhisattva," a practice which suggests the presence of strong feelings of spiritual solidarity and brotherhood deeply steeped in essential Mahāyāna models.

Typically, at the Lo-yang court the Buddha and Lao-tzu were both honored. This practice was not fortuitous; an early memorial (A.D. 166) addressed to the emperor includes a reference to the tradition that "Lao-tzu has gone into the region of the barbarians [north] and then has become the Buddha." This represents one of many efforts to bridge the discontinuities between traditional Chinese values and the new teachings. The same memorial, nevertheless, touches the deeper mood of the Buddhist ethic: "[It teaches] purity and emptiness; it venerates non-action [wu-wei]; it loves keeping alive and hates slaughter; it serves to diminish desires and expel intemperance."[4]

The social disturbances at the end of the Han extended into the period of the Three Kingdoms and Six Dynasties (A.D. 220-589). In the early part of the fourth century a series of "barbarian" (Hun) invasions and settlements in the north provoked a mass migration of Han gentry to the south. This long-lasting cultural split was important for the subsequent development of Buddhism in China.

In the north, amid the chaos of the times, Buddhism was a relatively calm oasis of religious stability closely integrated with the needs of the state. The Hun warlords found in Buddhism new means for religious legitimation and for establishing their own political identity on a wider cultural base which broke through traditional social fissures. The merit-making ethic was valuable for expiating past sins, gaining practical ends, and sanctioning desired social standards which still remained profoundly Confucian despite the decimation of the literati.

Buddhist advisers at court were hard-pressed to justify coercion and capital punishment. However, the common rationalization was that if the emperor did not personally administer punishment he was absolved from its bad karma. It was also necessary, of course, that his actions be just. An opinion on this matter was voiced by the great monk-magician Fo-t'u-teng (d. 349) who served as spiritual adviser to the royal court:

Worship of the Buddha on the part of emperors and kings lies in being personally reverent and inwardly obedient. . . . It lies in not being cruelly oppressive and killing the innocent. As for the rogues and reprobates who cannot be civilized or reformed, if they are guilty . . . they must be punished.[5]

Fo-t'u-teng—named "great jewel of the state" by the emperor—in many respects epitomizes the syncretic values of the northern court elite during this early period. He was of necessity specialized in magic, folk medicine, and

omen interpretation. His biographer tells us somewhat
apologetically that he practiced magic and avoided the
deeper aspects of Buddhist doctrine in order to convert
the rulers and help to relieve the suffering of the people.
He was also a prodigious missionary whose preaching was
aimed at mass conversion, especially among the "barbarian" tribes. This included the construction of nearly
nine hundred monasteries and temples during his ministry;
and there is a tradition that he established the first order
of nuns and introduced a fuller version of the monastic
rule.

Yet despite the universal thrust of Buddhist teaching
and its power to mitigate social and cultural divisions, one
consequence of its penetration among the "barbarians"
was its vulgarization in the eyes of upper-class minorities;
and equally serious was its occasional exploitation by
rebellious leaders, one of whom we find calling himself
"crown prince of the Buddha" and using messianic imagery. The instability of the northern dynasties is well
attested in the histories. In A.D. 349 no less than four
emperors were successively assassinated; and it is not surprising that some of Fo-t'u-teng's pupils fled the court
and sought new and more tranquil environments where
they could explore the deeper meaning of the teaching.

Among them was Tao-an (A.D. 312-385) whose work
exemplifies some of the characteristic features of this tran-
sitional period. His primary doctrinal focus was on the
Perfection of Wisdom materials, but his exegetical work
was deeply imbued with Taoist symbolism. The radical
implications of the Indian śūnya motif were adumbrated
by an ontology of "original nonbeing" or the "primal
undifferentiated" closely akin to Taoist metaphysics. And
he appropriated aspects of Mahāyāna cosmology by insti-
tuting the cult of the Bodhisattva Maitreya ("friendly

one"), the coming "messiah" of Indian tradition. Maitreya was also the patron saint of exegetes; the search for spiritual guidance in translation and interpretation must have been a deeply felt need. The effort to communicate Buddhist ideas through Chinese symbols had developed into a painfully self-conscious art—the *ko-i* ("matching concepts")—in which Taoist and Confucian philosophical vocabulary was employed in an increasingly elaborate scholastic framework. It presupposed not only a cultured familiarity with the classics, but often a dogmatic commitment to this interpretive technique. Some of the early masters felt considerable anxiety about the legitimacy of this enterprise, particularly since it played into the hands of Taoist and Confucian critics who could claim that Buddhism was really only a depraved foreign version of the pristine Chinese traditions. A typical response to these criticisms comes from the Buddhist master Mou-tzu (*ca.* A.D. 350?):

I have quoted those things [the Chinese classics] to you, sir, because I knew you would understand them. Had I preached the words of the Buddhist scriptures or discussed the essence of non-action, it would be like speaking about the five colors to the blind or playing the five sounds to the deaf.[6]

The vitality of Buddhism was in a very real sense always dependent upon the continued assurance of essential contact with the truths of the Buddha's teaching. Expedient adjustments to Chinese cultural forms, political needs and class interests were inevitable, but the striving to break loose from these chains can be seen in a number of areas. The master Chih-tun (A.D. 314-366) labored to penetrate the profundities of the *Perfection of Wisdom* materials: the polar bifurcation between being and nonbeing was difficult to overcome even where a sense of the deeper meaning of the "void," "emptiness," was somehow apprehended through its Taoist saturation. Chih-tun struggled with this problem: the "highest non-being" is a condition of spiritual perfection beyond conceptualization in which "being and non-being are naturally obliterated together; the low is no more since the high has been forgotten." This and comparable formulations indicate that the deeper meaning of the śūnyatā doctrine was becoming a working part of the philosophical repertoire.[7]

He coupled this insight with an equal interest in the cult of Amitābha (Amita) Buddha and the "pure land," which suggests an ever-widening popular social grounding of immense importance in the subsequent history of China and Japan. This combined interest in the philosophical and devotional aspects of Mahāyāna tradition is one of the most distinctive characteristics of the major schools which emerged and persisted during the following centuries.[8] With respect to lay ethics, the *Vimalakīrti Sūtra* appears prominently as a major source of inspiration because of its validation of the spiritual integrity of the ideal layman while still involved in the affairs of everyday life.

The most important event in the development of the integrity of Buddhist doctrine and institutional life during this period was state sponsorship of a systematic and remarkably disciplined translation of Buddhist texts under the supervision of the great Kuchan scholar Kumārajīva (A.D. 344-413). He was originally captured and held as the property of a local warlord who prized his charismatic and magical powers; but in his new capacity as chief translator and exegete for the state he not only introduced many new sūtras and commentaries, but retranslated some of the older sūtras with an expertise which did much to free these materials from earlier inaccuracies and their immersion in Taoist terminology.[9] The translations in-cluded works of the Mādhyamika (San-lun) school, in which he was particularly adept. The immense produc-tivity of this enterprise created a reservoir of source mate-rials which became the basis for later schools and set high standards of professional competence.

Despite these advances, there were countervailing forces at work. By the fifth century the entrenched status of the monastic orders—free from taxation and corvée—had resulted in internal abuses which from the viewpoint of the state disrupted their cultural and integrative functions. Almost from the beginning the monasteries had assumed economic responsibilities—at first nothing more than the distribution of charitable gifts and funds for the mainte-nance of the order, but in time many had accumulated vast wealth and properties. They were reputed to be sanc-tuaries for those who wanted to avoid secular obligations —including the transfer of land titles to avoid taxation—and as hotbeds of immorality and political subversion. The Taoist and Confucian elite did not fail to dramatize these accusations. As a result, efforts were made to break the power of the Saṅgha and to place it more directly under state control. A Caesaro-papist fusion of church and state was contemplated by the emperor of the northern Wei dynasty. It was suggested that he declare himself an incarnate Buddha and thus pre-empt the charismatic au-thority and power of the Order. In the long run the Saṅgha was able to resist this effort because the northern dynasties were inherently too unstable for a theocratic synthesis, but the emperor received the traditional honors and the title of Tathāgata from the court clergy.

More successful was the effort to control the Saṅgha by systematic reorganization and occasional persecution. A clerical bureaucracy in the Confucian pattern was superimposed on the monastic orders to guarantee internal regulation; and persecutions in the fifth and sixth centuries deprived the monasteries of much of their property, wealth, and personnel. All of this was mixed with sudden reversals of fortune as the Buddhists found themselves momentarily in favor at court again. In A.D. 454 the emperor endeavored to expiate the bad karma of the past by ordering the construction of the magnificent cave temples near Ta-t'ung.[10] These acts of coercion also had indirect but important consequences for the development of the Pure Land cult by intensifying the emphasis on eschatological symbolism and the need for salvation through Amita's power alone, and deepening its social grounding and universalism.

In the south the dynasties remained Chinese, and political and economic conditions were more stable. The primary cultural and ideological leadership was in the hands of the Confucian literati, though Taoism was strongly represented. Buddhist values continued to filter up through the higher social strata into the court itself; but the form they took was eclectic—dove-tailing with the elegant "pure conversation" (*ch'ing-t'an*) which expressed the refined and distinctive social status of an exclusive elite. Leading Buddhist monks were for the most part learned, Confucian-trained intellectuals prepared to deal equally with Taoist, hsüen-hsüeh, and Confucian teachings.

As the prestige of the Saṅgha increased an inevitable consequence was the recognition by the more powerful clans and the royal court of the unique cultural and spiritual authority of the most distinguished monks. So we find the emperor Ai (A.D. 362-366) inviting Chih-tun to the capital to expound the *Perfection of Wisdom* teaching. It is not recorded whether the court was particularly enlightened; but the increased prestige acquired by the

Saṅgha on these occasions resulted in many subsequent acts of official sponsorship and promotion. This development proved to be a mixed blessing. In the environment of the royal court the clergy and lay devotees were soon enmeshed in local intrigue and political factions. We find a classic indictment of these depredations in the words of the independent-minded general Hsü Yung (A.D. 389):

I have heard that the Buddha is a spirit of purity, far-reaching intelligence and mysterious emptiness. . . . But the devotees are vile, rude, servile and addicted to wine and women. . . . Monks and nuns crowd together. . . . They oppress and pillage the people, considering the collection of riches as wisdom. . . .[11]

And he urged that the clergy be appropriately humbled.

It is precisely at this point, and partly on this issue, that one of the most dramatic confrontations between the Saṅgha and the rulers of the state in China occurred. The antagonists were the military governor Huan Hsüan, who usurped the throne in 402; and the monk Hui-yüan (A.D. 334-417), whose personality, administrative skills, and scholarly labors are in a very real sense an epitome of early Chinese Buddhism. Hui-yüan was one of Tao-an's students who had taken refuge in the south from the civil wars and barbarism of the times. He built a monastery and school on Mount Lu, and sought to maintain his independence while at the same time synthesizing and enriching its symbolism with indigenous resources. His monastery was a richly Sinified center of Buddho-Confucian teaching. He was both an expert in the Confucian *li*—especially the mourning rights—and an ardent proponent of the Pure Land cult. To stabilize the lay ethic he stressed the moral efficacy of the karmic metaphysic and insisted that the laity observe the five relationships and the law of the land.

However, his rational accommodation of Buddhist teaching with Confucian norms was paradoxically mixed with a strong sense of the independent dignity of the monk over against the claims of the state cult. The military dictator Huan Hsüan was a man of culture who collected paintings and dabbled in Taoism and Buddhism, but he also was an outspoken anticleric when it came to court politics. He demanded complete authority over the Saṅgha, including the signs of appropriate homage due the emperor—specifically that the monks bow down before him in the traditional fashion. With remarkable courage Hui-yüan refused to conform to this court ritual. In a superb, quasi-prophetic treatise entitled *A Monk Does Not Bow Down before a King*, he argues that the monk does not lack loyalty or filial piety but has a higher loyalty to the universal Buddhist law to which all men are subject. The emperor must fulfill the role of the pious layman who supports the Saṅgha with his charity but does not seek to control it. His appeal is not only to the special status of the monk but to the unique spiritual role of Buddhism:

He who has left the household life is a lodger beyond the earthly world, and his ways are cut off from those of other beings. . . . Though inwardly they may run counter to the gravity of natural relationships, they do not violate filial piety; though outwardly they lack respect in serving the sovereign, they do not lose hold of reverence. Kings and princes, though they have the power of preserving existence, cannot cause a preserved creature to be without woe. But [the monk] understands how one terminates woe. . . . This is why the monk refuses homage to the emperor and keeps his own works sublime, and why he is not ranked with kings or princes and yet basks in their kindness.[12]

Huan Hsüan responded by granting this privilege.

From this position of leverage the monastic leadership of the Saṅgha in the south was often able to exercise a modicum of critical tension with the royal house. On the whole, however, the classical bifurcation between monk and layman prevented the formation of a lasting principle of secular, or lay, social criticism. Lay patrons were expected to conform humbly to the given political values of the state. Royal piety occasionally found expression in an ideal monarch, most notably in the emperor Liang Wu Ti (A.D. 502-549) who patronized the Sangha widely amid sensational acts of devotion. He was appropriately declared a bodhisattva. But in the last analysis the Sangha's power both in the north and in the south was dependent on the sympathy of the patrimonial monarch which might range from pious support to savage persecution depending on utilitarian need or personal whim.

Hui-yüan's interests included (as with his predecessors) the promotion of the Amita cult; and his activities in this area were so intensive that he is traditionally regarded as the founder of the Pure Land school in China. This attribution is historically untenable, but the vow which he and his disciples took together before an image of Amita, to seek rebirth in the "pure-land" was recorded; and the drama of the event and related ceremony is therefore of paradigmatic significance for the subsequent history of the cult.

In addition to these devotional pursuits, Hui-yüan meticulously studied the Vinaya, demanding rigorous adherence to its provisions; he also maintained a deep interest in the more refractory philosophical problems of the tradition. His letters written to the northern master Kumārajīva often consist of disarmingly frank questions about the most difficult issues: How can the theory of discrete entities (the atomic components of conditioned phenomena) be harmonized with the theory of the "emptiness" of all phenomena? How can one attain complete nonexistence by an endless division of existing things?

Where is the borderline between being and nonbeing?
These letters are remarkable for their evidence of an insatiable desire to learn; and for the most part they seem
to have pressed Kumārajīva beyond his capacities (or
willingness) to give incisive answers.[13]

The conquest of the south and the unification of China
under the Sui dynasty (A.D. 581-618) was followed by a
deliberate effort on the part of the Sui rulers to use the
three major religions coordinately to promote cultural
unity. Buddhism not only supplied the religious imagery
but also the ideology behind the conquests of the founder
of the Sui. He deliberately drew on the Buddhist traditions
about King Aśoka and justified the use of force by infusing
it with cultic imagery: ". . . we regard the weapons of
war as having become like the offerings of incense and
flowers presented to the Buddha . . . ." Of value also was
the psychological conditioning of the army through Bud-
dhist-inspired emphasis on the immortality of the soul
and the trivial consequences of bodily wounds and death
itself.[14]

The Buddhist monasteries, patronized by wealthy aristocratic families, were important links between upper and
lower status groups. They implemented a pietistic economic justice by redistributing wealth and other commodi-
ties to the poor—a rational contribution in a time of low
economic mobility. State supervision was tight. Monks
were required to hold government-approved certificates
of ordination and submit to the supervision of a state-
appointed Vinaya master.

The monastic orders were highly disciplined corporate
bodies governed by the rules of the Vinaya through which
all monks of whatever sectarian persuasion were supposed
to receive their training and ordination.[15] The eschatological and messianic bodhisattva cults—often that of

Maitreya—were regarded as potentially seditious, since they had occasionally provided imagery congenial to rebellious movements. Popular devotionalism, however, on the whole performed a valuable service for the state, since it promoted a mood of intimate piety which could effectively sublimate outer-directed hostilities. At an even more diffuse popular level there were the hermit-shamans, the recluse "monks" of uncertain affiliation who practiced folk magic, exorcism, medicine, and fortune-telling on behalf of the great bulk of the illiterate population.

The major Buddhist schools—now emerging in full strength—provided varied outlets for personal choice, intellectual and spiritual satisfaction. These schools did not develop primarily out of institutional schism or sectarian dissent. Instead, they were formed around the teachings of one or more of the received Indian sūtras, commentaries, and doctrinal systems expounded in China by a master and his designated successors. Confronted as they were with the immense profusion of source materials, the practical goal was to reconcile and harmonize the texts. Some of the schools were based dominantly on the literature of the Indian philosophical schools—as with Mādhyamika and Vijñānavāda. But others, T'ien-t'ai ("Heavenly Terrace") and Hua-yen ("Flower Garland"), had no specific Indian institutional counterparts except that implied by the key sūtras around which they catalogued other sources. Membership was necessarily limited to a relatively select literate group, though Pure Land was inherently capable of wide popular diffusion.

The most marked institutional feature common to the schools was their patriarchal lineage structure suggested by the Chinese term *tsung*, which really means "clan" although it is often translated "school" or "sect." The integrity of the master-pupil succession was steeped in an atmosphere of filial piety and the clan model. However, their doctrinal etiology was distinctively Buddhist even where Chinese forms and methods were superimposed. The biography of the T'ien-t'ai patriarch Hui-ssu (A.D. 515-576) and the work of his disciples is a distillation of the syncretic character of this school. In his youth he felt the call of the *Lotus Sūtra*, to save all mankind; and after an arduous period of ascetic discipline and meditation he had a vision of Maitreya which confirmed his missionary calling. The eschatological symbolism seemed tangent to the conditions of the times, and his preaching was driven by the notion that this last and most degenerate of ages urgently demanded conversion and total commitment for salvation. He moved south, as had so many others, to escape the civil wars, and there on Mount T'ien T'ai founded his school.

His disciple Chih-i (A.D. 538-597) developed the doctrine through massive systematization of Buddhist materials —Hīnayāna and Mahāyāna—centered around the *Lotus Sūtra*.[16] The specific goal was to harmonize all Buddhist doctrines in one omnipotent teaching, combining philosophy and meditation like "the two wings of a bird." Its metaphysical system affirmed (1) that all phenomena are empty and void but (2) nevertheless have a provisional being which constitutes the working reality of existence. It is this paradoxical quality of phenomena which is (3) the true Mean, the Absolute. Out of this essential unity emerges a vast cosmology: the buddhas, bodhisattvas, gods, spirits, human beings, and lower phenomena. In this way the doctrine—"the harmonious threefold truth" —sanctified an immense spectrum of philosophical, cultic, and ethical symbolism—including the hierarchical order of the natural world and socio-political institutions.

The Hua-yen school centered on the Indian *Avataṃsaka*

("flower garland") *Sūtra* which was deeply imbued with idealist metaphysics. The doctrine asserts that all phenomena are manifestations of an essential noumenon (tathatā) paradoxically identified with the "void." Other ontologically vital symbols were employed to illumine the spiritual dynamics and harmony of the universe, and the teaching deliberately strives to rationalize and ameliorate the appearance of phenomenal conflict and worldly strife. The master Fa-tsang (A.D. 643-712), who was for many years the chief Buddhist philosopher of the royal court, states in his *Golden Lion* sermon that "the All is the One, both alike having no permanent nature; and the One is the All, for cause and effect clearly follow each other. . . . They are completely compatible with each other and do not obstruct each other's peaceful existence." The search for intellectual clarification was tied to a pervasive need for a sense of integration and the rudimentary coherence of all natural and social forms.[17]

The new political stability under the Sui extended into the T'ang dynasty (A.D. 618-907), and Buddhism underwent a remarkable institutional flowering. The Empress Wu (A.D. 684-705), to whom Fa-tsang addressed the *Lion* sermon, took the Buddhist title *cakravartin deva* ("divine empress who rules the world"). The T'ang capital was a great center of Sino-Buddhist art and ceremonial, gilding the power of the royal court with suitable charisma and aesthetic beauty. The provinces and villages were dominated by Buddhist temples and staffed with clergy tending to the personal affairs of the faithful and simultaneously reinforcing broader solidarity.

By the eighth century the diffusion of Buddhism had in many ways broken through many of the old particularisms and created a relatively unified Buddhist culture, moderating the severity of the ferocious penal codes and promoting many charitable works. The great festivals of the Buddha's Birthday and the Feast of All Souls were fused with indigenous and local cultic traditions. Pious donations assumed the proportions of public work projects with obvious economic advantages—the building of new roads and bridges, hostels, and free hospitals.

The bodhisattvas of unstinting love—especially Amita and Avalokiteśvara (Kuan-yin), embodied in omnipresent icons and images—saturated the wider ethos. The Pure Land school had from the very beginning shown a special power of social penetration and inclusiveness for the reasons already outlined. But in the hands of the masters of the sixth and seventh centuries it was grounded on a special technique for personal salvation which became so diffusely popular that it seems to have been rather more a pervasive religious culture than a school. Specifically, it was asserted that rebirth in the heavenly "pure land" could be attained simply by pious repetition of Amita's name, and that through this means even the most reprehensible sinner could be saved. Amita's love and power would suffice.[18]

The rationale for this shift from monastic meditation to the new form of devotion came first from the patriarch T'an-luan (A.D. 476-542) and later from Tao-ch'o (562-645). Their reasoning was guided by the old Indian theory of historical degeneration: since the human situation is so totally depraved it is impossible to expect most men to follow the "path of the saints"—the techniques of monastic asceticism and meditation, "Buddha contemplation." Instead, Amita has made available the "easy path" through "Buddha-invocation." Tao-ch'o, originally a T'ien-t'ai monk, justified this teaching with a characteristically sophisticated and comprehensive argument:

The bodhisattva encourages all beings to be reborn in the Pure Land. But does this not combine love with craving? The answer is that the teachings practiced by the bodhisattva are of two kinds. One is the perception of the understanding of emptiness and perfect wisdom. The second is full possession of great compassion. . . . The bodhisattva is always able subtly to reject existence and non-existence. . . . This is the birth of no-birth into which the superior gentlemen enter. . . . But there are middle and lower classes of bodhisattvas who are not yet able to overcome the world of external forms, and who must rely on faith in the Buddha to seek rebirth in the Pure Land.[19]

The diffusion of Pure Land teaching was widely promoted by Shan-tao (A.D. 613-681) a tireless evangelist, artist, and musician whose prodigious reputation was carried to Japan where he was regarded as a worldly manifestation of Amitābha himself. The antinomian potential of the teaching was carefully guarded: the master Tz'u-min (680-748) insisted on rigorous adherence to moral principles, whether one practiced meditation or invocation—a welcome corrective from the viewpoints of the state and those concerned with the reputation of the Saṅgha. During the T'ang era Pure Land was popularly accepted through all social strata from emperor to slave. It infiltrated the cultic life of many other sects and persisted long after the neo-Confucian reforms had toppled most of the other great Buddhist schools.

The most remarkable synthesis of Chinese and Indian Buddhist values was achieved in the Meditation School (Ch'an, Zen). Though Ch'an history for the early period is shrouded in legend, its leadership appears to have developed a unique meditative technique driven by the conviction that true enlightenment comes from a salutary insight into the identity between the self and the essential Buddha-nature, namely, that one's true nature is not and never has been different from nirvāṇa itself. In theory this was not significantly at variance with the "emptiness" (śūnyatā) and idealist traditions; saṃsāra and nirvāṇa are "void" and "illusory" and therefore the same. Enlightenment is a consequence of a profound intuition of this truth. What was different, however, was that the Ch'an yoga emphasized nondiscursive, practical, and naturalistic media for attaining this insight. The somewhat legendary founder of Ch'an, Bodhidharma (*ca.* A.D. 500?), is reputed to have asserted that his doctrine was unique because it pointed "directly to one's true nature" without the burden of traditional textual studies.[20] The teaching was maintained through a master-disciple relationship founded rigidly on the principle of patriarchal succession—in many respects far more rigorous than the authoritarian models of the other schools. The "authority" principle was not an expedient form of hierarchical order, but a basic factor in the learning process, in the living confrontation between teacher and pupil through which the essentials of the teaching were conveyed.

Its most distinctive features appear first clearly in the seventh century when the school split into two main sects: the school of "gradual enlightenment," which stressed the importance of meditation within the framework of traditional textual study; and the school of "sudden enlightenment." The latter ultimately followed a line of development in which all residuals of abstract intellectualism, traditional texts, and dogmas were abandoned in favor of new techniques designed to break routine patterns of thought and conceptualization ("word drunkenness") which inhibit intuitive insight and the realization of the Buddha-nature latent in every man.

These events and their institutional consequences are outlined in an oft-cited autobiographical passage from *The Platform Scripture of the Sixth Patriarch.* Here Hui-neng

(A.D. 683-713), the reputed founder of the "sudden enlightenment" school, tells how his special insight gained
him succession to the patriarchate: Another student had
written a verse which said:

> Our body is the tree of Perfect Wisdom,
> And our mind is a bright mirror.
> At all times diligently wipe them,
> So that they will be free from dust.

Hui-neng countered with the verse:

> The tree of Perfect Wisdom is originally no tree.
> Nor has the bright mirror any frame.
> Buddha-nature is forever clear and pure.
> Where is there any dust?[21]

This gentle formulation strikes directly at the symbolic
bifurcation between essence and existence inherent in the
"otherworldly" goals and elaborate techniques of the traditional yoga, and it suggests the profound iconoclasm of
radical Ch'an, deliberately setting out to shatter the formal
conceptual tools which more and more appeared to be a
limitation and not a means to enlightenment. In this respect
Ch'an, like Pure Land—with which it seems to differ so
radically—is a protest against the immensely detailed symbolic scholasticism of the philosophical schools. Moreover,
there is an egalitarian thrust: Hui-neng is depicted in the
tradition as an illiterate and uncultured kitchen scullion
whose intuitive brilliance fractured all social amenities. To
the accusation that he was a "barbarian" from the north
he says: "There is neither north nor south in Buddha-
nature. In physical body, the barbarian and the monk are
different. But what is the difference in their Buddha-
nature? . . . Perfection is inherent in all people."

This untutored upstart was duly selected by the Fifth

Patriarch Hung-jen (A.D. 601-675) to assume the patriarchal robe; he then had to flee for his life because of
the jealousy of the other monks who suddenly found their
hard-earned spiritual prerogatives and status dissolve. It is
doubtful that Hui-neng was as uncultured as tradition
makes him out to be. But the story is a paradigm of the
special values of his school. Knowledge of the sūtras,
erudition, and intellectual accomplishments often remained
important prerequisites, and cultured sensibilities were
presumed. But these are of value because they are the
preconditions for the experience of discarding them as
one gains spiritual and intuitional competence. Consequently a talented disciple with native spiritual capacity
should not be burdened with these superficialities. Hui-
neng's successor, Shen-hui, was, nevertheless, a learned
and highly articulate preacher who talked a great deal
about the noncognitive essentials of enlightenment:

> "Absence of thought" is the doctrine.
> "Absence of action" is the foundation.
> True Emptiness is the substance. . . .
> The mind is originally without activity;
> The Way is always without thought.
> No thought, no reflection, no seeking, no attainment.
> No this, no that, no coming, no going.[22]

This is the basis for a spontaneous apprehension of the
Buddha-nature, as the adept recognizes "his original face"
and is freed from the anxieties of striving and self-doubt.
The content of this experience cannot be adequately ver-
balized, but is expressed in a new sense of integrated
self-confidence and security: "the original nature has no
wrong, no disturbance, no delusion" (Hui-neng).

There was no question in Shen-hui's mind that the
framework of patriarchal authority was the institutional
bulwark which guaranteed the maintenance of the deep-

est truths amid this freedom from traditional doctrinal restraints:

> The [patriarchal] robe is the testimony of the Law and the Law is the doctrine represented by the robe. There is only the transmission through the robe and the Law; there is no other way.[23]

Ch'an techniques were quite diverse, but are most notably expressed in the *kung-an* (*kōan*) or "public case" method. This body of material, passed down by the masters, consists of short paradoxical questions or riddles designed both to block routine intellection and to provoke a salutary experience of illumination if the conditions be right. They are immensely varied, but their deeper rationality often seems quite apparent, especially where they dramatize nonduality in an appropriately startling way:

> A monk said "Your disciple is sick all over, please cure me." The Master said "I shall not cure you." The monk said "Why don't you cure me?" The Master said "So that you neither live nor die."[24]

In order to liberate the disciple from conventional paralysis, deliberate eccentricities were cultivated: the Buddha was apparently blasphemed ("dried dung," "a bag of beans," "three pounds of flax," "a chatterbox"). Physical beatings and even bodily mutilation administered by the master were occasionally practiced; the violent jolting of the psyche through any means, including assaults on the body if the student seemed to require it, was regarded as a legitimate if highly specialized practice. In many respects Ch'an practices are analogous to the Tantric legitimation of "abnormal" behavior as the most effective means for breaking the bonds of spiritual ignorance and frustration.[25] But for the most part antinomian tendencies were held in check by the Confucian ethic and the monastic rule. This "lightning" technique was practiced chiefly by the Lin-chi (Rinzai) masters—one of the two main Ch'an sects which persisted after the eleventh century. The other sect—the Ts'ao-tung (Sōtō)—encouraged textual study and systematic meditation as well as the kung-an.

Ch'an retained much of the traditional monastic discipline though in modified form. The essential teaching was communicated without ecclesiastical or textual encumbrances, which proved helpful not only in facilitating missionary mobility but also in surviving the persecutions which destroyed the edifices, property, and literature of the more traditional schools. The Meditation masters frequently required their disciples to do manual labor—an active asceticism—which violated the mandates of the Vinaya but also undercut the traditional model of the routinized yoga and passive withdrawal. In its practicality and simultaneous validation of the natural world in the very act of transcending it, there is much of native Chinese naturalism and mystical Taoism. The schools exercised considerable influence on the arts and aesthetic values by stressing the inner spiritual depths of the natural form and act, and consequently Ch'an culture always had a broad social grounding.

Buddhism reached its zenith in China as a state-supported institution during the eighth century. But in the latter part of the T'ang it began to weaken. The main factors in this decline were the rise of Taoist political power in the royal court and the renewed importance of Confucianism among the gentry class, including the restoration of the bureaucratic examination system under new Confucian leadership. Internal rebellions and barbarian pressures on the frontiers contributed to the collapse of the great family systems on which Buddhism had relied.[26] Equally important was the fact that once again the Buddhist temples and monasteries had become entrenched centers of irrational economic and political power which from the viewpoint of the state outweighed their cultural contributions. In A.D. 845 a massive persecution was instituted during which—according to the emperor Wu—over 44,000 temples and monasteries were demolished and their properties confiscated, releasing millions of acres of land and their laborers. Monks and nuns were compelled to return to productive lay occupations.

This disastrous de-institution of Buddhism in the late T'ang was capped in the Sung (960-1279) by the Neo-Confucian reform which effectively broke the back of Buddhist intellectual pre-eminence in philosophy and placed Confucianism on a new and metaphysically satisfying base. It represents an attack on the Buddhist worldview while at the same time appropriating from Buddhism not only much of its deeper spiritual orientation but also a new concern for the individual and questions of personal meaning.[27]

From the perspective of the great Neo-Confucian thinker Chu Hsi (1130-1200), the Confucian sage can attain a profound spiritual insight which leads to salutary enlightenment. This new image encroached on the unique role of the Buddhist monk. Specifically, the Neo-Confucian attack on Buddhism was in two directions. First, there was an assault on the idea that since the world is in constant change and flux it is nothing but meaningless suffering and illusion. On the contrary, all change shows order and permanence in the larger process if not in particular things. Second, there was an attack on the idea that the world is empty, and that one should turn away from outer sensations and progressively realize the artificiality not only of the world but of the mind's assertion of the independent reality of the world and the mind. On the contrary, instead of turning from it, its principles must be investigated, its norms discovered as the basis for the active correction of worldly imperfection and the actualization of essential spiritual truths.

By the end of the Sung dynasty Buddhism had lost much of its intellectual social grounding.[28] The Mongols supported Tibetan Lamaism and Tantrism as did the Manchus (1644-1911) for political reasons, but the long association of Buddhism with "barbarian" dynasties contributed to the general revulsion against it which characterizes much of later Chinese intellectual thought. Monasticism continued, and Ch'an and Pure Land remained strong, but under the closest government supervision. The Buddhist clergy were often relegated to the service of popular religious needs and competed with the Taoist shamans for pre-eminence in magical therapy. Their main role was to pray for the souls of the dead, while the Taoists were specialists in the exorcism of demons and sickness. Individuals seeking their aid were not classified as Buddhists or Taoists, but simply as Chinese consulting specialists who were often without congregations. A residual of Buddhist lay piety remained in several secret societies— most notably the White Lotus, vaguely related to the Maitreya cult, which served largely as a social and economic guild with little in the way of real devotional fervor or religious universalism.[29]

3. Southeast Asia and Tibet

THE MISSIONARY MOVEMENTS of Theravāda Buddhism into Ceylon and Indochina, and of Tantric Buddhism into Tibet, hide similarities which reveal the deeper facets of Buddhist universalism despite stark contrasts in doctrine and practice. In both cases Buddhism provided the religious base not only for evolutionary advances but for long-lasting societies. In both cases it was introduced as a state "church" under favorable ecological, cultural, and political circumstances by rulers who controlled relatively small, homogeneous land areas. These rulers saw in Buddhism an opportunity to innovate and to provide a broader religious base for legitimation and social integration. With respect to the church-state relationship, however, in Tibet this evolutionary movement finally took the form of a theocracy based on a unique rationalization of Mahāyāna and Tantric incarnational theology; while in Ceylon and Indochina the Theravāda—with its two-class division between celibate monk and layman and its orthodox version of the classical tradition—maintained a structural distinction between church and state which had important consequences: the king was lay "defender of the faith" working cooperatively with the superior charismatic and educative power of the monastic order which provided state chaplains, missionaries, and teachers who could cross traditional boundary lines, and create a new cultural milieu. The specialized performance of these tasks by the Saṅgha and the structural distinction between church and state also allowed for the formation of secular bureaucracies and of executive and administrative controls not bound to a sacerdotal hierarchy.

In coordination with King Aśoka's political and ideological universalism, Theravāda missions reached Ceylon and possibly western Indochina by the end of the third century B.C. In Ceylon—reputedly missionized by Aśoka's son, Mahinda—it was instituted as the official religion of the state, and became the chief citadel of Theravādin orthodoxy.[1] Though its diffusion was slower in Indochina, where Mahāyāna, Hindu and Chinese values were strongly entrenched, the prevailing culture was in time predominantly Theravādin. In all cases its introduction facilitated the development of more highly differentiated polities by freeing societal resources from their embeddedness in traditional communal and ascriptive ties.

This *rapprochement* between the state and the monastic leadership of Theravāda did not take place without significant changes in the values and institutions of the ancient Indian Saṅgha, particularly those factors which had precipitated its earlier sectarian instability. Some of these modifications may have been promoted by King Aśoka at the third council in Pāṭaliputra (*ca.* 250 B.C.) in order to stem the schismatic disturbances to which several of his inscriptions and Buddhist tradition attest. But others—including *ad hoc* administrative and legal restraints—were developed later in Ceylon and Indochina under direct state supervision: first, the radical independence of the individual monk was placed under routine controls by introducing a hierarchy of scholastic distinctions and grades of perfection based on seniority, knowledge of the texts, and the monastic Rule. Some of these modifications are to be found in later portions of the Vinaya. This adjustment provided more real space and time for the individual monk to perform worldly tasks devoted to lay needs without being stigmatized as a spiritual weakling.

Second, monastic authority was redefined in a way which sets it off strikingly from the early mandate attributed to the Buddha interdicting centralized ecclesiastical control. We find new rationalizations of the legitimacy of patriarchal authority. A uniform line of successors to the Buddha's authority based on the traditional "succession of masters" was used to justify hierarchical control of the monastic order approaching that of a unified church and backed by the power of the state.[2]

Finally, a doctrinal orthodoxy was established. The key text is the *Kathāvatthu* ("Refutation") reputedly promulgated under King Aśoka's supervision and contained in the Abhidhamma. It declares 252 non-Theravādin teachings "heretical" without bothering to argue the issues at stake in depth. The Abhidhamma is, in general, a collection of scholastic classifications, unburdened by the deliberately cultivated philosophical subtleties and esotericism of the Mahāyāna and Tantric traditions. Where opportunities exist for innovative philosophical exploration, orthodox closure tends to intervene.

These lines of authority were reinforced by the definition of other essential forms. The councils of Rājagṛha, Vaiśālī, and Pāṭaliputra were approved as officially binding. At the fourth Theravādin council (25 B.C.) the threefold canon of scriptures was finalized and established as the basis for a uniform ecclesiastical law. In this newly stabilized form, Theravāda was located on a solid institutional and doctrinal ground from which it could more effectively serve the goals of the state. The ethical precepts and the other rational socioeconomic and political teachings set generalized standards for interpersonal and intergroup relations at all levels of society.

In Ceylon, the Saṅgha was partially fused with existing feudal institutions, forming a monastic landlordism preempting over one-third of the land. But it also taught necessary technical skills and norms, and provided a wider sphere for social consensus and political legitimation. As in India, one of the great advantages of the new religion was that it did not simply displace the old animistic and magical beliefs. It assimilated and frequently reinforced them so that they continued to function at the local level but under a hierarchy of new educative controls which vastly extended the range of individual social awareness and political loyalties.

These innovations are dramatized in the Chronicles of Ceylon with stories about the conversion of the indigenous deities and demons, most of whom are of the animistic or archaic Hindu variety associated with local communal values. We are told how the power of the Buddha, embodied in the missionary preaching, transformed these local trouble-makers into dutiful disciples loyal to the wider values of the new Buddhist state formed under King Tissa (247-207 B.C.): "myriads of snake-spirits were converted to the Three Treasures and moral precepts." After this in short order, so goes the tradition, the monastic Orders were formed, the doctrine was propagated throughout the island and the people "converted."[3] It was probably only in and around the capital city of Anurādhapura that all this took place, but the king could not have failed to recognize its larger potential.

Hindu culture is presupposed. The presence of Brāhmanic institutions, including the priesthood and caste, is well attested in the Chronicles and it is notable that caste and certain Brāhmanic rites persisted. One of the most significant features of the earliest monastic centers is that they were deliberately oriented to pre-existing ascriptive social distinctions—one for the nobility (the Issarasamanika) and one for the upper-class commoners (the Vessagiri).[4] This represents a departure from the old Indian model, and was certainly the basis for preliminary social stabilization. Equally important was the alignment of this new monastic elite with the city-state hierarchy, an advantage which King Aśoka did not have. Conspicuously absent was a large and entrenched Brāhman priesthood. The Brāhmans appear to have been relatively few in number and limited to specialized cultic needs. The most crucial fact is that Buddhism provided new integrative power a rich variety of specifically exoteric symbols including an appropriate selection of Buddha-relics and a branch from the Bodhi Tree reputedly sent by Aśoka himself. These became important objects of popular devotion and shared communal awareness.

Royal legitimation was tied to this new symbolic repertoire. Possession of the Buddha's alms bowl and other essential relics was a prerequisite for legitimate monarchial succession, and the personal piety of the king and his court was an imperative. Power struggles within the patrimonial court persisted, including usurpation by Tamil invaders. But the grass-roots social penetration of Buddhism was such that few monarchs could afford to be without it. Acts against the doctrine or the physical property of the Saṅgha were rated high treason. The model of royal piety sustained by the tradition presents sensational examples of this custom: we are told that the Tamil king Elāra (2nd century B.C.) accidentally ran a wheel of his chariot into a stupa and "though this had come to pass without his intending it, yet the king leaped from the car and flung himself down upon the road with the words 'Sever my head with the wheel.'" His repentance and suitable payment for damages were sufficient.[5]

The Saṅgha could bring immense moral power and popular sentiment to bear against a monarch of whom it disapproved. One of the most salient acts of disapproval which could be used against any troublesome layman was the old practice of "turning over the alms bowl" (*pattanikkujjana*)—simply refusing to accept alms. This silent act was a form of excommunication which had the effect not only of isolating the offender from the community but of formally stigmatizing him as a social and political criminal. In addition, the monks were adept in traditional magic and folk medicine, an immensely rich synthesis which always was a major source of monastic authority well into the modern era.

In contests over royal succession the Saṅgha could apply pressures in favor of one potential heir over another. There are examples of armed troops assembling in the monastic precincts and of monks suddenly emerging as soldiers to support an approved contender. The Hindu Tamil invasions did much to transform Theravāda into a national ideology: King Duṭṭhagāmaṇī (101–77 B.C.) put a Buddha relic on his royal spear and asked monks to come with him into battle (a violation of the Vinaya) against King Elāra, whose piety had not withstood the test of time, particularly in view of his foreign nationality. After Duṭṭhagāmaṇī's victory he is represented as suitably distraught, "since I have caused the slaughter of millions." But he is consoled by the monks as follows:

From this deed arises no hindrance in thy way to heaven. Only one and a half human beings have been slain here by thee, O lord of men. The one had come unto the Three Refuges and the other had taken unto himself the five precepts. Unbelievers and men of evil life were the rest, not more to be esteemed than beasts. Thou wilt illumine the doctrine of the Buddha in many ways, therefore dispel care from thy mind.[6]

This rationalization is evidence of the intimate relationship between "national" political sensibilities and Buddhist values.

All of this, as it stands in the Chronicles, was paradigmatic for church-state relations as they continued to develop. However, patrimonial authority did not always favor ecclesiastical stability. There were schismatic movements within the Saṅgha itself—many promoted by royal favoritism. The most important monastery was the Mahāvihāra—a bastion of Theravādin orthodoxy. Under royal auspices a new monastic center—the Abhayagiri—was instituted in the first century B.C. The picture we have of this new center and its teachings comes from the hands of Theravādin divines who ultimately had it suppressed as heretical, so it is difficult to separate fact from pejoration. But it is clear that the Abhayagiri was receptive to new teachings from India which sound distinctively Mahāyānist. This is clearly the case with one called Mahāsuññavāda ("doctrine of the great void")—which must have promoted a form of Śūnyavāda, though the description is imprecise: it held to a docetic teaching in which the Buddha was regarded as a nonhuman teacher; and since he never existed in physical form the conclusion was drawn that physical gifts to the Saṅgha were useless and without merit. The potential effect of this teaching on

Theravādin economics must have seemed ominous. Later, another sect called the Vājiriavāda is described as being popular among "foolish and ignorant people because it was practised secretly as a mystic teaching." The name and description suggest Tantric esotericism possibly of the Vajrayāna variety, which must have been regarded as a horrible depravity by the Theravādin elite.[7] Other sectarian movements are attributed to the Abhayagiri; and though the descriptions are often vague, the issues at stake are clear: it was a liberal outlet for heterodox teachings and practices. The doctrinal and institutional threat to the Theravāda was very real.

This conflict lasted for centuries, exacerbated by patrimonial strife in the royal court in which the two opposing monastic orders were often involved. In the face of continued Tamil invasions and recurrent civil war, several monarchs actually sought to muster Hindu legitimation. We read that King Mahinda II (A.D. 772-792) in addition to being an ardent Buddhist "restored many delapidated temples of Hindu gods and gave the Brāhmans delicious foods such as the King received."

Efforts to "purify" the Saṅgha and establish the orthodox teaching as absolutely authoritative were only provisionally successful. But several important events are recorded: in the fifth century A.D., under royal auspices, the great Theravādin Indian scholar Buddhaghosa came to Ceylon to confirm the orthodox doctrine and explicate the teaching with commentaries designed to establish its authenticity as the only legitimate form of Buddhism. And in the eleventh century, after a period of serious decline, King Vijayabāhu appointed a supreme head (*Saṅgharāja*) of the monastic orders and promoted lasting reforms—including valid ordination rites obtained from Burma. The position of the Saṅgharāja, a primate working directly with the state, was a model for ecclesiastical authority in Indochina as well; and we find occasional exchanges between Ceylon, Burma, and Thailand in mutual support of Theravādin integrity. In addition, administrative law books were introduced by royal fiat which regularized and enforced bureaucratic controls.[8]

The final victory of Theravāda in Ceylon lies in its deep penetration among the masses and its fusion with national interests in the face of the long history of invasions from India identified with Hindu and Mahāyāna culture. And the Saṅgha also possessed a rational clerical bureaucracy, and a simple and morally upright teaching which in the long run provided the most stable base for social integration.

On the Southeast Asian mainland Burma, Thailand, Cambodia, and Laos also became major centers of Theravādin culture. Northern Vietnam, however, was dominantly under the influence of Confucian and Chinese Buddhist values, while Indian Mahāyāna and Tantric teaching made deep penetrations not only on the mainland but into Java and Sumatra.

One of the most striking examples of the evolutionary power of Theravāda in Indochina is to be found in Thai history. Though the Thai case cannot be considered entirely representative, it provides an effective illustration of the larger pattern. Some preliminary observations on the pre-Buddhist cultural background are necessary here. Prior to the introduction of Indian religions, the mainland of Southeast Asia was inhabited by Austronesian (Malayo-Polynesian) peoples, distributed spottily along the major rivers and seacoasts. Their economies were based mainly on wet-rice agriculture, and there were other staples which indicate conditions well beyond minimal subsistence levels. Yet despite this economic potential it appears that no centralized states of significant proportions had developed. The largest social units were tribal and village-based.

Alliances were only occasionally formed for warfare or economic needs—fishing and minor commodity exchange. Political power was located in clan lineages with relations between village members based on kinship ties. The religions were primitive, in the sense that objects of worship were fused with many discrete natural phenomena and with clan totemic objects. These institutions served to maintain a high level of local solidarity but a very low level of generalized political authority and class differentiation.

It can hardly be regarded as coincidental that with the introduction of Hindu culture, shortly before the beginning of the Christian era, a number of relatively large kingdoms seem to have evolved, the most powerful of which in time was the Khmer empire (*ca.* 7th-15th centuries A.D.).[9] Brāhmanic Hinduism, with its esoteric ritualism and principles of caste stratification, was the first religion widely and successfully institutionalized. Caste, with its large-scale ascriptive hierarchies, is a semiuniversal structure which at least transcends narrow tribal provincialism and kinship ties, and can create an environment in which a wide range of heterogeneous social units can be brought within a coherent system of laws, with minimal dislocation of ancient customs. The principal Khmer political unit was the feudal province, and traditional villages retained a great deal of autonomy. In A.D. 802, King Jayavarman II was installed on the throne in the fashion of the Hindu divine king, and sacerdotal authority was invested in a hereditary Brāhman elite. The polity was primarily of the feudal-vassal type with some bureaucratization. Local chiefs retained their traditional affiliations while acknowledging the suzerainty of the paramount sovereign.

But this system had several disadvantages. First, within

the scope of the Hindu pantheon and related cults, it was possible for would-be contenders to the throne to claim legitimation by appealing to the power of an alternative Hindu deity and its supporters, and thus polarize political resistance. Despite many efforts at cultic synthesis the Khmer suffered from a long series of internal struggles. This included usurpations in the name of Mahāyāna deities and incarnate Buddharājas.[10] Though Mahāyāna culture found expression in the great Buddhist monuments at Angkor Thom, it did not achieve widespread social penetration. Bodhisattva status was reserved chiefly for the elite. This was not only because the Mahāyāna cults were adjusted to the predominant Brāhmanic hierarchies and "divine kingship" theology, but because it lacked social grounding on a numerically large and disciplined monasticism like the Theravāda with genuinely exoteric and popular commitments. Second, under pressure, caste stratification tended to collapse back into the local ascriptive and kinship structures of which it was comprised; and the masses could not share in the esoteric values of the court. In short, there were many lines of potential social and political cleavage which were not bridged by Brāhmanic or prevailing Mahāyāna resources. Consequently, though the Khmer empire was characterized by the development of a semibureaucratized feudal system, it was wracked by internal dissension and political weakness.

An indication of the inherent limitations of this system is to be found in the historical fact that the Khmer empire succumbed to the Thai invaders from the north, who formed new polities on the remains of the northern Khmer provinces. And, most significantly, the Hindu blueprint was dropped in favor of Theravāda Buddhism. Theravāda had already proved itself on the mainland: The old city-state of Thanton in lower Burma—the earliest major center of Theravādin teaching on the mainland—was annexed in the eleventh century by King Anawrahta of Pagan in upper Burma. The tradition relates that his urgent request for Theravādin texts and clergy from Thanton had been rebuffed, so he invaded lower Burma and carried off thirty sets of the canon along with a large monastic retinue. Pagan became the major center for the propagation of Theravādin teaching, and was the capital of the new Burmese state. The king is also reputed to have driven out Vajrayāna Tantric adepts, though there is evidence that Hindu and Mahāyāna culture in general persisted alongside Theravāda.[11]

The Thai monarchs followed the same model, and it is clear that the early Thai kingdom which emerged in the mid-thirteenth century was supported by the Theravādin Saṅgha. The records of King Rāma Kamheng (*ca.* 1275-1300), show that he instituted a clerical hierarchy headed by monks sent to Ceylon for fuller training under the prestigious Sinhalese elite. As he and his successors extended their borders, the Saṅgha helped to socialize and acculturate conquered non-Thai groups. Legitimation for royal authority was based on the patrimonial contractual theory, with the king serving as the chief Buddhist layman, setting the example for all through his piety, but without divine cultic status. The concept of lay "defender of the faith" established an image which was eminently popular; with respect to spiritual status and access to the essentials of the teaching, the king was theoretically no different from any commoner. Kings who tried to use incarnational theologies for usurpation or Caesaro-papist legitimation were on the whole successfully resisted and deposed by Theravādin-sponsored opposition. Rāma Kamheng's "democratic" paternalism is much in evidence in his inscriptions, which, like King Aśoka's, were designed for popular consumption and reveal a new kind of communalism far removed from the Hindu cultic "divine king" model:

On days other than those on which the [Buddhist] precepts are recited, King Rāma seats himself on this stone slab, and presiding over the assembly of nobles and dignitaries discusses with them the affairs of state. . . . If commoner, noble, or chief falls ill, dies and disappears, his ancestral home, his clothes, his elephants, his rice granaries, his slaves, his family plantations are inherited in their entirety by his children. If commoners, nobles, or chiefs are in disagreement [the king] makes a thorough inquiry and then decides the affair for his subjects in accordance with equity; he does not connive as the thief or receiver of stolen goods. If he sees the rice of another he is not indignant. . . . In the entrance to the gate (of the palace) a bell is hung up. If a subject of the realm has any trouble or any matter that distresses him within or torments his heart, and which he wishes to declare to his prince, there is no difficulty; he has only to ring the bell that is suspended there. Whenever King Rāma hears this appeal he questions [the plaintiff] concerning his case [and decides it] according to the right.[12]

The structural differentiation between church and state provided a wide area for rational secular developments. Under the later monarchs, most notably King Trailok (1448-1488), it allowed the formation of a civil bureaucracy which became the long-lasting basis for Thai administration up to modern times. Specialized departments were set up under the titular rule of royal princes with the actual administration performed by civilian officials. The Saṅgha was headed by a patriarch, appointed by the king, who sat on the royal council. He coordinated the activities of the Saṅgha with the needs of the state, maintaining an important sphere for communication between the royal court and outlying provinces.

Although hereditary ascription remained an important integrative principle including discriminatory laws and penalties, the system was considerably opened to individual achievement because access to the civilian bureaucracy and the religious hierarchy was based on free education provided by village monks. In addition, all young males were expected (as they still are) to spend at least several months living as novices in training with the monastic community; and the Saṅgha taught skills and values necessary for official positions.

The "householders" ethic stressed the autonomous rights and responsibilities of each member of the conjugal family, and partially freed it from consanguinal ascription, thus increasing the potential for individual mobility. Promotion in the bureaucratic hierarchy was based significantly on moral prestige derived by adhering to the precepts and other merit-making acts.[13]

The mediation of the Saṅgha at the village level was an important factor in minimizing bureaucratic oppressiveness, since the presence of monks obviated the need for detailed bureaucratic supervision and meddling at local levels and encouraged the amicable settlement of personal and communal strife. In general, the Theravāda represented a qualitative advance over the primitive and archaic systems which preceded it. This was true throughout Indochina wherever the Saṅgha attained dominant institutional strength.

Cambodia, the heir to the once great Khmer empire, was in time a major Theravādin center—a change which was already underway in the late thirteenth century. A Chinese visitor appears to describe the Theravādin monks accurately as "men who shave the head, wear yellow clothing and leave the right shoulder uncovered."[14] Only shortly thereafter the last Brāhmanic Sanskrit inscription was incised, and a later inscription of this era states that "the nobles and high dignitaries, the Brāhmans and wealthy merchants gradually ceased to occupy the first place in society, and astrologers and physicians lost their prestige." This formulation reflects massive changes in traditional sociocultural patterns, in part related to growing political and economic conflicts between the main centers of city-state power: Pagan, Angkor, and the Thai capital at Ayuthia.[15] A major precipitant was the Mongol invasions. Mongol armies took Pagan in 1287 and applied pressure to the other major states. The Thais moved south and sacked Angkor in 1389; and the great city with its magnificent architectural monuments was later abandoned to the jungle.

In this situation of endemic conflict the deeper and increasingly dominant substratum of Theravādin culture appears to have provided the principal source of solace and solidarity. The defeated Khmer monarch was named Dhammāsokarāja ("the Righteous King Aśoka") after the traditional paradigm of royal Buddhist piety. This apparently peripheral fact is nevertheless a symbol of the general penetration of Buddhist values which sustained communal life at lower levels beyond the demise of particular monarchs and dynasties, while patrimonial and political warfare persisted. The fusion of Theravādin teaching and local traditions centered in the economically self-sufficient village had a remarkably stabilizing effect. Primitive guardian spirits and demons—the *nats* in Burma and the *phi* in Laos, for example—were incorporated into the Buddhist pantheon, and village monks were proficient in local magical and medicinal arts. The "rites of passage" —of birth, adolescence, marriage, sickness, and death— and the ever present round of yearly communal festivals were managed under the aegis of the local pagoda. Personal devotion often took the form of merit-making gifts in labor and goods for the maintenance of the monks and monastic buildings. It was always possible for the great bulk of the rural population to remain within the protection of the village precincts while the major urban centers were wracked by patrimonial warfare and military siege.

On the northeast coast of the mainland—in Vietnam— a very different cultural situation prevailed. Social and political institutions were developed mainly under Chinese influence. As early as the second century B.C. the area around the Red River was regarded as a province of the Chinese empire, and bureaucratization, cemented by Confucian values, was underway by the second century A.D. Chinese remained the official language until modern times. Though Buddhism was strongly represented—chiefly by Chinese Mahāyāna in the form of Pure Land and Ch'an —the religious environment was highly syncretic, including Taoism in various amalgams with Buddhist and traditional shamanistic practices.[16]

There is an old saying that "when the times are peaceful the Vietnamese are Confucians, but when the times are troubled, they are Buddhists." Apart from the special valance of Buddhist values for dealing with the most intimate problems of religious meaning, an important general factor was that by comparison with Chinese imperialism, Indian institutions arrived largely free of charge. Native chiefs and populations did not have Indian values forced on them. Rather, they were presented with cultural tools and religious means which they could employ as suited their particular needs.

Indonesia was an early recipient of a broad spectrum of Indian values, largely through long-standing commercial and political contacts with India and southern Indochina.[17] Hinduism and Mahāyāna institutions were much in evidence by the fifth and sixth centuries A.D. in Java and Sumatra. The Kingdom of Śrivijaya included Malaya and parts of Java, and by the seventh century A.D. its monarchs had promoted the development of a major center of Buddhist studies at the capital city Palembang which may have included Theravādin materials. There is also evidence of Brāhmanic and Tantric institutions, though the historical data are too limited to form an accurate picture of the range of social penetration.[18] One of the most superb examples of Buddhist art and architecture is the Borobudur stupa erected in the eighth century by the Śailendra rulers in central Java. This immense edifice, now in serious decay, is ornamented with several thousand stone reliefs and statues integrated to represent the various stages of enlightenment.[19] At the height of its power the empire included Java, Sumatra, and Malaya, with significant encroachments into southern Indochina. It is probable that Śailendra civilization was, at least in part, a model for the Khmer (Cambodian) achievements represented most dramatically by Angkor. But like Angkor, Śailendra architectural remains reflect the special interests of a powerful centralized government and a privileged elite using economic resources and a large force of full-time laborers and artisans to gild autocratic power with Buddhist piety.[20] Though the evidence is slim, we may surmise that the popular social grounding of Mahāyāna was shallow by comparison with Theravādin culture in Ceylon and on the mainland for the reasons noted above—that is, the absence of large-scale exoteric and bureaucratized monasticism.

The mixed Buddhist-Hindu civilization in Indonesia lasted until the fifteenth century when Islam finally gained political ascendancy and suppressed the infidel religions. Muslim hegemony was in part the result of its inherent capacity to cut through the archaic social fissures which had not been effectively bridged by the Hindu and Mahāyāna cults. Aggressive political and mercantile forces stemming chiefly from Malacca brought the "unity of Islam" to the attention of indigenous rulers ("the trader was the most common missionary.")[21]

In ancient Tibet—as with the major Indochinese states —Buddhism provided equally important ecclesiastical support and evolutionary guidelines, but chiefly through Mahāyāna and Tantric values, and under cultural conditions which resulted in a unique synthesis. The economy was agricultural and pastoral, with little in the way of commercial exchange and mobility. The native religion— though historical reconstruction is difficult—seems to have been a magical animism (Bönism) marked by a labyrinthian demonolatry controlled by Bönist shamans who specialized in manipulatory magic, necromancy, divination, and exorcism.[22]

It has often been observed that Tibet's climate, terrain, and the generally harsh conditions of existence were major factors in the structuring of this archaic symbolism. The isolation, forbidding mountain ranges and precipitous gorges, the waterless deserts, violent wind storms and icy winters—all these dramatized the natural precariousness and awe-inspiring conditions of human life.[23] But it is also true that the animistic pantheon and related shamanistic practices reflect the widely prevalent matrix of very archaic Indo-Iranian and central Asian traditions elevated to an apotheosis of horror: the walking dead, vampires, hundreds of malevolent spirits, each with a specialized talent to inflict sickness, torture, and death. Even the Tibetan hearth god, the sacred companion of every home, was a choleric spirit. Trivial neglect—a hair in an offering of butter or a pot that boils over—could provoke remorseless punishment. The archaic Bön religion, nevertheless, provided a logical framework within which the irrational contingencies of life could at least be ascribed to recognized causes, to active if often demonic forces which were subject to appropriate aversive and therapeutic rites. The religion also provided sanctions for the maintenance of social norms and a loosely structured solidarity largely centered in extended clan lineages and local chiefs. The rationalization of monarchial authority, though very limited, appears in mythopoeic form, with appropriate rituals including animal and even human sacrifices. A retinue of professional oracles and soothsayers provided some innovative leverage over traditional patterns in the absence of even craft literacy.[24]

In the seventh century A.D., there was a movement toward political and military consolidation under the first of a series of strong monarchs who opened Tibet to long-range cultural and economic influences from China and India. Political alliances were formed through polygamous state marriages, including two royal princesses from Nepal and China who are reputed to have brought Buddhism into the sphere of court life.[25] King Srong-btsan sgam-po (620-649) was apparently quick to see the cultural advantages of the new religion and the resources of the great civilizations from which it came. Indian written characters and grammar were introduced by members of the court who studied with Mahāyāna monks in Kashmir, and—though the tradition is uncertain—Buddhist temples were constructed in politically strategic districts. There is no reliable evidence that the royal house at first tried to displace the old Bön priesthood; but this preliminary affiliation with Buddhism was strengthened in the eighth century by an influx of refugee monks from politically disturbed areas in central Asia. Monastic centers were built to house them, and royal patronage assumed the proportions of overt state support. The privileged status of this new elite and its access to the royal court was enhanced by the fact that King Mes-ag-tshoms (704-755) married a Chinese princess of the T'ang dynasty whose ardent Buddhist piety like that of her predecessors is well attested in the chronicles. This political and cultural alliance between the Tibetan and Chinese courts served to elevate the status of the Tibetan royal house along with a few aristocratic families, but at the expense of the old provincial nobility. Buddhist legitimation was a factor in royal consolidation, and it is not surprising that the Bön priesthood soon aligned itself with the old nobility. This polarization resulted in a long series of struggles which in the end not only undercut the monarchy but weakened secular political controls and prepared the way for the final triumph of the Buddhist theocracy.

In the late eighth century King Khri-srong (756-796), after suppressing opposition in the court (the prime minister was buried alive), sent emissaries to India to procure the services of the famed Buddhist master Śāntirakṣita at the University of Nālandā—for definitive missionary work, it was hoped. However, his teaching stressed highly rational forms of Mahāyāna ethics and philosophy, and had no rapport with the beliefs of the masses. His presence antagonized the Bön priests and provincial chiefs who forced his expulsion when the local demons and gods duly announced their displeasure. The traditions relate that when Śāntirakṣita was asked to return he advised the king that he was incapable of dealing with the evil Tibetan gods, and instead recommended "the greatest sorcerer in India—master Padmasambhava."

The biographical data for Padmasambhava are immersed in myth and legend.[26] They nevertheless reveal a symbolic architecture which readily explains his success. He is represented as a master of many religious, philosophical, scientific, and magical techniques—from the grossest forms of shamanistic necromancy and black magic, through sexual Tantrism and folk medicine, to the most refined aspects of Hīnayāna and Mahāyāna doctrine (including also Brāhmanism, Jainism, and "other teachings"). The capstone of his proficiency was probably the rich flux of Vajrayāna esotericism, but he was by no means limited to it. Through the legendary and ill-historical biographies we can perceive the presence of an intellectual and religious genius whose monumental synthetic powers were formed in the pan-cultural matrix of north India, and whose zeal was aroused by the almost unlimited possibilities for religious syncretism and missionary conquest in Tibet. The legendary model of overwhelming spiritual and worldly power which he represents was developed in the later Tibetan traditions of the rNying-ma-pa sect which is attributed to him. It is nevertheless a paradigm of the cultural transformation of Tibet itself in this early period, and so he is above all Tibet's most ancient culture-hero.

In the traditions we find him at the outset dignified by a suitably miraculous birth, royal status, and prodigious athletic skill. After his conversion to the religious life he spent his first years of training imbibing secret teachings which gave him magical control over the forces of death and the demonic world. As "God of the Corpses" he meets the abysmal evils and rapacious ferocity of life with equally violent but transforming spiritual power. One brief legend conveys as no routine biography could the kaleidoscopic symbolic and ritual power of the Tantric and shamanistic practices in which he was steeped; of his confrontation with a powerful king "hostile to religion" it is said:

He deprived the king and all the men among the unbelievers of their bodies, or means of sowing further evil karma; and, magically transmuting their bodies he drank the blood and ate the flesh. Their souls he thus liberated and prevented from falling into hells. Every woman whom he met he took to himself, in order to purify her spiritually and fit her to become the mother of religiously minded offspring.

Then, as the "Eternal Comforter of all Beings," he conquers "all the most furious and fearful evil spirits, 21,000 devils male and female" and "all good and bad demons controlling oracles in Tibet." And he subsequently restores them all to life "making them to serve the cause of religion."[27]

All of this represents a legendary distillation of the major cultural assault which wrenched Tibet loose from its archaic roots. The symbolism is deeply steeped in shamanistic rites of initiation and magic—all part of the Tantric repertoire; its main theme is the conquest and transformation of evil and fear in the service of the Buddha and mankind.

The probable historical facts put Padmasambhava and his retinue in Tibet in 747 for a missionary stay of about two years (though the traditions vastly extend it). His unique status in the royal court is evidenced by the fact that he requested and received one of the king's wives, increasing the number of his female consorts to five. The description of his sensational success in converting the Bön spirits to Buddhism is somewhat tempered by the tradition that he was later grieved by the apostasy of the native gods who were moved to revolt several times. This reflects the tide of political and religious resistance which culminated in anti-Buddhist revolts in the ninth century. But the crucial facts are, first, that Tantrism was a salient medium for the conquest of the archaic pantheon. Its success was due in part to the inherent grass-roots appeal of the theistic and magical symbolism to those already steeped in the indigenous religion. But compared with Bönism it provided a more highly differentiated and psychologically liberating system of beliefs and practices. Second, Padmasambhava's teachings were socially grounded on the rNying-ma-pa school and its various subsects, which continued to promote and further rationalize the cult. His efforts were followed by the ordination of Tibetan monks, and later by the arrival of other Mahāyāna and Tantric masters.

The literate Buddhist clergy were armed with a charisma which, in time, overwhelmed local chiefs, sorcerers, and demons alike. The native deities were subordinated to the superior power of the Buddhist pantheon, and moral standards were reformed and universalized through the karmic theodicy. Typically, many primitive indigenous practices were assimilated and placed under a suitable socializing hierarchy. Religious resources later included a wide range of additional Mahāyāna and Hīnayāna texts as well as the Tantric materials, and the monasteries became centers for systematic translation and study.

Bönism was overtly suppressed. The priests were given the choice of converting to Buddhism or reverting to the status of taxpaying laymen, but many simply conformed to the externals while retaining their old commitments and others found refuge in outlying provinces. Moreover, members of the Bön elite responded to the challenge of Buddhism by reconstructing their teachings to conform with major structural and doctrinal features of Buddhist tradition. In the long run the somewhat ironic effect was to move Bönism into a relatively peripheral position, which it nevertheless retained in strength despite efforts to eliminate it altogether.

Although the Tibetan historians tend to shape early events to highlight later achievements, one event recorded for the later part of Khri-srong's reign is particularly important. An internal dispute developed in the court between the Chinese and the Indian Buddhists. The former were apparently influenced by early Ch'an teachings, and the latter by Mādhyamika and Yogācāra teachings espoused by Śāntirakṣita, who had returned briefly in the wake of Padmasambhava's successes. An open debate was held at Lhasa in which the Chinese master is represented as arguing that enlightenment is a sudden and intuitive experience unburdened by ethical and intellectual striving, the ideal medium being "inactivity." In refutation the Mahāyāna master insists that his adversary's doctrine leads to nothing more than worldly torpor analogous to drunkenness. Intuition of the "void" and final enlightenment can only be the result of systematic moral discipline, that is, intellectual and ethical mastery over the self and the world. The Mahāyāna party is reported to have won the argument and the Chinese were banished. The most striking feature of this church "council" is that its outcome favored a doctrine likely to facilitate rational moral and social controls.[28] It supplements the Tantric rites and represents the deliberate selection of those aspects of Buddhist teaching relevant to the construction of an elite ideology with positive institutional consequences, one which also appears later as the source of major reforming movements. However, it is equally true that, as in the case of Indochina, Chinese culture, including its religions, was often identified with imperialist ambitions, while Indian values were not.

Khri-srong's immediate successors continued to support and develop Buddhist institutions, but by increasing repressive measures against the recalcitrant Bön priests and old nobility. This ended in a massive revolt in which the throne was usurped by the Bönist party and Buddhism formally proscribed. The Tibetan historians describe it as a situation of massive decline. A small elite found refuge in outlying provinces where the integrity of Buddhist tradition was maintained. And from this sanctuary a strong resurgence developed—most importantly under the aegis of a provincial ruler, Ye-shes-od, who joined the monastic order, assuming the epithet "royal monk." This event, which in a sense presages the theocratic synthesis of later centuries, was followed by a large-scale revival. The monk-king is represented as a man of moral rigor, an exponent of the Vinaya, Mahāyāna philosophy, and a reformed Tantrism. His dynastic successors pursued the same course; and in A.D. 1040 they engaged the services of the great Indian Mahāyāna master Atīśa from Vikramaśīla University.[29] He arrived in Tibet prepared to undertake the training of a new cadre of monks for missionary activity in central Tibet itself. His teaching was imbued with the most exalted array of classical Mahāyāna values, as represented in his book *Lamp for the Way of Enlightenment* written especially for this occasion. It stresses the characteristic moral and spiritual disciplines necessary for long-range missionary goals, and rates as spiritually inferior those who strive only for their own self-perfection and neglect the spiritual welfare of others.

His mission was supported by a wealthy layman with contacts in central Tibet who, with Atīśa's pupil Brom-ston (1005-1064), also helped to institute the bKa-gdams-pa ("authoritative word sect") centered around Atīśa's teaching. This decisive grounding among aristocratic and mercantile groups gave him access to major lines of communication—even in Lhasa itself. Tantric symbolism and mysteries were employed to support the salient philosophical and ethical teachings. Atīśa was also a devotee of the Tantric goddess Tārā, Avalokiteśvara's consort, and he gave much thought to the role of the devotional cult. His success was certainly due in large part to his own genius; but equally important was the support of the affluent laity and families among the nobility for whom Bön archaisms and Tantric excesses were debased and dehumanizing. It is interesting to note that Atīśa was persuaded to come to Tibet only after a large payment in gold by the Tibetan emissaries, which he then donated for the maintenance of Buddhist holy places in India. It seems probable that this outlay of hard cash was taken as an index of the economic and political viability of the whole enterprise. We find that Atīśa's school played an important role in the development of the later theocracy because its doctrinal and disciplinary rigor was a major model for subsequent reforms and innovations.

The Buddhist restoration in the eleventh century provided the general framework for the development of a diverse range of schools, including the techniques of Vajrayāna. The legends about its earliest masters are paradigms of mystical antinomianism. But the reforming impulse associated with the work of Atīśa found its way into the mainstream of this tradition as well, and there is no more striking example of this than the life of Mi-la-ras-pa (1040-1123), Tibet's greatest religious poet and in many respects its most sublime saint.[30] He began his spiritual apprenticeship—so goes the tradition—by learning to kill and destroy through the black magic of the shamanistic tradition. In order to expunge his bad Karma, his teacher Mar-pa (1012-1097) treated him with deliberate brutality for many years before grudgingly revealing the innermost secrets of the doctrine. Out of this ordeal Mi-la-ras-pa emerges as a paradigm of immense courage and monumental heroic strength (precisely the rational function of the ferocious authoritarian master-pupil model). And with all this behind him he turns deliberately to the loftiest ascetic and ethical pursuits. His poems contained in *The*

Hundred Thousand Chants reveal a man of love and compassion filled with a profound sense of the beauty of life amid its pervasive transience:

> This joyous site of fields and hills in
> A land of grassy slopes and flowers of many hues,
> With glades where fair trees dance. . . .
> I am joyous in the clear light of the Void,
> At its many ways of appearance,
> At its immense variety.

His instructions to his disciples are full of moral rigor:

When practising the rites that you've learned,
Do not use this power to vanquish demons,
For if you do your inner self will rise up as a demon,
And if this occurs, the superstitious practice of the common
   people will prevail. . . .
Abandon what you know is wrong,
Evil conduct and lying speech,
Pocketing fees at funeral rites
And giving advice only to please.[31]

One legend of profound cultural significance is the story of Mi-la-ras-pa's decisive defeat of a leading Bön priest in a contest of magical power. It symbolizes the final and historically real victory of Buddhism over its old rival in later centuries, though Bön practices persisted in many areas, most often in syncretism with Buddhist tradition itself.

Another school of central importance in Tibetan political history is the Sa-skya-pa. Its doctrines were centered on a modified Tantrism which included a rich magical repertoire and cultic worship, principally of the Bodhisattva Mañjuśrī. Celibacy was not a requirement and the hierarchy of the school became a hereditary patriarchate. Its economic base was substantial, including extensive land holdings and consequent political power. By the thirteenth century it controlled large parts of Tibet, with the abbot serving as the *de facto* monarch. Legitimation was provided in part by an incarnational theology in which the priest-king was regarded as the worldly manifestation of Mañjuśrī.

By far the most pivotal event in the history of this school —and in many respects for Tibet itself—was the alliance of this sect with the Mongols. In 1246 a representative of the school was invited to the Mongol court where he is reputed to have cured the reigning prince of a serious illness. The prince's conversion to Buddhism is represented as a suitable expression of pious gratitude; but it also seems clear that the Mongol ruler saw the religion as a potent source for cultural integration, and magical and social controls independent of the Chinese political authority. The prince and his great successor, Kublai Khan, formally supported the supreme hegemony of the Sa-skya-pa over the whole of Tibet. However, the association of this school with Mongol military power and its privileged position drove other monastic institutions into defensive political and economic alignments which ended in open hostilities. By the end of the fourteenth century there were severe social disruptions, including pitched battles between various monastic fortresses and their armies. The inevitable consequence was a shift in monastic values toward those more congenial to the temporal struggle. Although the Tibetan historians may have exaggerated this degeneration in order to highlight the achievements of the later reformers, it was indeed a "time of troubles," including resurgent primitivisms, compulsive magic, and widespread abrogation of monastic discipline.

However, the models of perfection exemplified by the Atīśa and Mi-la-ras-pa traditions persisted, and with the collapse of the Mongol empire these inner resources found new creative outlets and produced a remarkable reforming movement. The monk Tsong-kha-pa (1357-1419), who initiated this reform, emerges as a genuine prophetic figure.[32] He was a specialist in Mādhyamika philosophy, logic, and the rigors of the Vinaya. He was a prodigious student, and as a teacher soon began to attract a wide following, founding a new school, the dGe-lugs-pa ("Virtuous sect"), also called the "Yellow Church." The color yellow signified his purifying reforms in contrast with the old Tantric practices of the "Red Church," and new monastic centers were founded to accommodate the growing cadre of his followers. He saw himself not as an innovator but as a follower of the pristine tradition represented chiefly by Atīśa's school. His avowed goal was the elimination of Vajrayāna abuses, the restoration of monastic celibacy, discipline, and ethics. His reconstruction of the Tantric system was based on Atīśa's reforms—eliminating overt eroticism and placing the magical technocracy under the control of rational ethics—and is best exemplified in his book *The Stages of the Great Way to the Occult Sciences.* Daily activities in the monasteries were regulated so that the monks had little opportunity for self-indulgence. The cult and its symbols were purged of former abuses, including the main temple at Lhasa. The archaic New Year celebrations were incorporated with the Buddhist Feast of Intercession for the well-being of all creatures, and monks of the Yellow Church exercised police powers during the various festivals to assure appropriate social controls.

The general atmosphere is one of massive reform verging on puritanical excess, but in fact the vitality of the devotional cults and the esoteric mysteries of the Tantra were retained. Other concessions were made, one of the most interesting being the inclusion of selected Red Church Tantric specialists—usually married men—into the reformed monastic faculties. This, in fact, served to accelerate the partial collapse of Red Church solidarity.

The sudden success and wide social grounding of Tsong-kha-pa's teaching during his lifetime was certainly related to the decline of Mongol power and the resurgence of a sense of political independence centered on autonomous cultural reconstruction; however, the fact that it should take this purified form rather than those provided by the more archaic and earthly native traditions is revealing. It underscores the deep human need for personal experience of stabilizing ethical values in the face of social and psychic chaos, and the search for a higher discipline which brings freedom from primitive fears and a wider sense of human fellowship. The subsequent institutional accommodations which inevitably followed the reform in no way detract from its extraordinary achievements.

The hierarchical rationale and consolidation of the Yellow Church was furthered by Tsong-kha-pa's successors. In the old Red Church, traditional authority was maintained by hereditary patriarchal succession, since celibacy was not required and the monks were encouraged to take spouses. This was a factor in the undermining and final destruction of the secular monarchy. By contrast, since celibacy was a prerequisite in the Yellow Church, legitimate patriarchal succession was maintained through a unique rationalization of incarnational theory: each of the chief lamas in the clerical hierarchy was held to be a worldly incarnation of a divine bodhisattva, reborn as an infant in a lay household shortly after the lama died.[33] His spirit transmigrated into the newborn child whose legitimacy was determined through elaborate rites of divination. The child was then trained in the monastery, under rigorous supervision. This seemingly arbitrary system was in fact remarkably rational. First, it assured the maintenance of the sacred space-time continuum in the succession without reinforcing familial and clan autocracies. Second, because it was based on the absolute justice of the karmic theodicy, it was eminently popular. Theoretically any Tibetan family might be the blessed recipient of the bodhisattva's divine favor. Third, it was open to carefully planned manipulation, since the rites of divination could be adjusted—chiefly through the state oracle—to accommodate a suitable family, and the young boy could then be carefully supervised as he matured.

The metaphysical base of this ingenious system was further routinized by an emanational theology in which the original creator Buddha (Ādibuddha) produced, interpenetrated, and controlled all subdeities and forms of institutional authority. This was not only a soteriological hierarchy but a paradigm for the organization of the state, representing the order of the ecclesiastical bureaucracy and the organic participation of various subsects and all the people in the spiritual power of the chief lamas. In its final form the two principal emanations were embodied in the Dalai Lama (Avalokiteśvara) who served as temporal ruler, and the Panchen Lama (Amitābha) who was authoritative in doctrinal matters.

After Tsong-kha-pa's death several events were of particular importance: In the late sixteenth century a new political and religious alliance with the Mongols was formed. The tribes had lapsed back into their old shamanistic practices and tribal warfare. At the specific request of the Altan Khan their "reconversion" was accomplished with paradigmatic grandeur by the third Dalai Lama who, somewhat in the fashion of Padmasambhava, "conquered" the archaic Mongol war gods and demons amid energetic proselytizing in route.[34] The old cult was formally banned, and the tribes were incorporated—not without coercion—

into the Yellow Church. After the Grand Lama's death in 1588, the experts in the art of incarnational divination discovered his spiritual embodiment in the grandson of the Altan Khan. As the fourth Dalai Lama he took up residence in Tibet. This potent alliance disturbed the Chinese rulers, who feared a resurgent Mongol nationalism. They obtained an agreement that the Dalai Lama should thenceforth be incarnate only in Tibet. However, high incarnational lamas at lower levels in the ecclesiastical bureaucracy were divined in both Mongolia and China.

The fifth Dalai Lama stands out as a man of extraordinary talents who performed the final act of theocratic consolidation. Scholar, poet, and executive genius, he expropriated the few remaining properties of the Red Church, suppressed an attempted restoration of the Bön religion, and annexed the independent provinces.[35] He ignored the law of celibacy, designating his own son as regent, the temporal administrator of the church. He is described as having delved into the old Tantras and cultic practices of the Red Church, doubtless finding sufficient legitimation there for these and other innovations.

The regency system which he initiated became the structural backbone of this monolithic ecclesia. It was not a hereditary office, nor was it subject directly to incarnational divination. Regents were appointed from candidates among the high incarnational adult lamas in the four major monasteries around Lhasa. Theoretically the regent governed only until the infant chosen as Dalai Lama came of age. But the inner weakness of the pure incarnational tradition, which required that autocratic power be placed in the hands of a young man not always competent to bear it, meant that exceptions had to be made, some of which were genuinely tragic. The sixth Dalai Lama was apparently given to drink and erotic excess ostensibly within the old Tantric tradition. A conspiratorial council decided that the spirit of Avalokiteśvara had abandoned his body. His supporters were murdered, and the Dalai Lama was carried forcibly into exile by the Mongol army where he died. The Chinese put up their own pretender to the throne and took military control of the state. Lhasa itself was sacked. Under the seventh and eighth Dalai Lamas temporary peace was restored and reforms initiated. But subsequently the Tibetan regents in league with the Chinese envoys retained absolute power; and somehow, none of the youthful Dalai Lamas from the ninth to the twelfth incarnations came of age.

Amid all these political disturbances at high levels, the integrated religious life and pervasive social controls of the great tradition sustained the larger community in a remarkably stable framework. The popular cultic and festival life of the community was imbued with symbols which accentuated the sacred coherence of Tibetan history, its ethical and institutional evolution.

The rites of the annual Padmasambhava celebrations were dramatic re-enactments of his life and his conquest over death and the old demons of Tibet, including the approved forms of sorcery and magic; the victory of the Yellow Church and its values was celebrated in public dramas which visually depict the defeat of the Red Church and the Bön priests. The innumerable prayer wheels were never simply mechanical merit-makers or means of aversive magic; they were omnipresent signs of the spiritual energies of Buddhism shared by the whole community.[36]

The integral relation between the economic life of the community and the monastic centers tended to place special weight on the spiritual significance of such commonplace matters as taxation and voluntary offerings. The taint of secular commercialism and the threat of profane degradations were bled off through a rich pattern of giving and sharing. These practices tended to transform the acquisition of personal material wealth into sources of merit which reinforced a wider sense of communal solidarity in addition to personal prestige. This was particularly the case with the fine arts; religious paintings, sculpture, architecture, dance, drama, and music—all received immense stimulus from a sense of communally shared piety.[37]

4. Japan

JAPAN HAD NOT participated independently in the cultural revolutions of the first millennium B.C. For Japan, as for Tibet and Southeast Asia, this transition occurred much later—in the sixth and seventh centuries under the impact of Sino-Buddhist values and institutions imported from Korea.

Prior to the arrival of Buddhism, Japan was dominated by a warrior aristocracy organized in large consanguinal clans controlling peasant and artisan villages. There was very little social structure that was not embedded in local kinship patterns and sanctioned by a primitive, proto-Shintō religion.[1] In A.D. 552 the king of one of the independent Korean states seeking to cement economic and political relations with Japan sent an embassy along with a Buddha image, priests, and texts. He commended Buddhism to the emperor in a way which suggests its growing pre-eminence under the Sui rulers in China:

This doctrine is amongst all doctrines the most excellent, but it is hard to explain and hard to comprehend. Even the Duke of Chou and Confucius could not attain a knowledge of it. This

doctrine can create religious merit and retribution without measure and without bounds . . . so that a man might satisfy all his
wishes in proportion as he used them. . . . Every prayer is ful-
filled and naught is wanting. Moreover, from distant India it
has extended hither to Korea, where there is none who do not
receive it with reverence as it is preached to them.[2]

The emphasis on the health-giving, magical powers of
Buddhist doctrine is combined with an unmistakable image
of its universalism and its capacity to bridge political and
social fissures. Though it was highly valued for its magical
therapy and prestige as the symbol of the great civilization to the west, its resonance with the political and ideological needs of the times must have been apparent from
the very outset. Furthermore, it was the bearer of the
deeper reservoir of Chinese culture: the arts and sciences,
medicine, and Confucian political and social values. It is
significant that the emperor and one of the leading aristocratic clans closest to the court—the Soga—embraced
Buddhism in the face of bitter resistance from more traditionally minded clansmen who had a political stake in the
provincial conservatism of the indigenous religion.

This conflict, plus the inherent problems of translation
and dissemination, at first effectively blocked the diffusion
of Buddhist values.

It was not until the seventh century that the real breakthrough was initiated by one of the greatest figures in
Japanese history, Prince Shōtoku (573-621). Shōtoku assumed the regency at the age of nineteen when there was
growing strife between the leading clans over imperial
succession. The emperor had been murdered, and the
empress Suiko (592-628) reluctantly agreed to take the
throne with the assistance of Shōtoku, whose native brilliance is chronicled with an appropriately exaggerated
assertion that "he was able to speak as soon as he was

born and was so wise when he grew up that he could attend to the suits of ten men at once and decide them all without error."[3]

In the midst of this public and private strife Shōtoku converted to Buddhism as a layman, and with the assistance of Korean monks he began to reconstruct his society on the broader ethical and cultural base provided by Buddhist values. The innovative significance of his conversion is suggested by a statement traditionally attributed to him: "The world is empty and vain—only the Buddha is true." In this ecstatic affirmation of the fundamental principle of world-rejection, he appears to have taken the first step in the process of liberating his society from the paralytic burden of the archaic institutions which surrounded him. His reconstructive enterprise was spelled out in a new ideology embodied in a royal proclamation which is recognizably a fusion of Buddhist universalism and Confucian ethics.

Sincerely reverence the Three Treasures—the Buddha, the Law and the Monastic orders [which] are the supreme objects of faith in all countries. Few men are utterly bad. They may be taught to follow it. . . .

When you receive the imperial commands fail not scrupulously to obey them. The lord is Heaven and the vassal is Earth. . . . The ministers and functionaries should make decorous behavior their leading principle. . . . Every man should have his own charge, and let not the spheres of duty be confused. . . .

Wisdom is the product of earnest meditation. . . . Let us cease from wrath and refrain from angry looks. Nor let us be resentful when others differ from us. For all men have hearts and each heart has its own leanings. Their right is our wrong, and our right is their wrong. We are not unquestionably sages, nor are they unquestionably fools. Both of us are simply ordinary men. How can one lay down a rule by which to distinguish right from wrong? For we are all one with another wise and foolish, like a ring which has no end.[4]

These few passages from the larger text reflect his concern for the mitigation of clan hostility within the wider framework of Buddhist sensibilities while at the same time strengthening the model of centralized political authority.[5] Shōtoku actually ruled from the monastery, availing himself of new legitimation and innovative leverage provided by the highly organized and literate monastic order. He sent embassies to China to bring back the resources of Chinese civilization which became the basis for later innovation, most notably the Taika reforms (646) and codes based on T'ang law, land systems, and bureaucratic principles.[6] At the same time he began to compile traditional ancestral myths underlying the clan genealogies, a project which culminated later in *Kojiki* and *Nihongi*.

A direct assault on the clan system would doubtless have spelled disaster to his larger goals. In the end, clan barriers proved unassailable, and Japan remained essentially a patrimonial state with only the partial beginnings of a true bureaucracy. Political developments were primarily in the direction of a clan-based feudalism and patrimonial hierarchy. However, Shōtoku's innovations were an immense stride forward, and in historical retrospect they have no equal until modern times.

Later in the seventh century power struggles within court persisted, but the assimilation of Chinese culture continued. Buddhism played a remarkably varied role in political legitimation: in 672 the emperor Temmu justified his usurpation of the throne with passages from the *Golden Light Sūtra* which affirmed that personal religious merit rather than hereditary standing was the real source of the "divine right" to rule. The sūtra also outlines a program of religious and political control based on the idea that the propagation of Buddhism will assure personal and social health without limit:

If any king upholds this sutra and makes offering on its behalf, I [the Buddha] will purify him of suffering and illness, and bring him peace of mind. I will protect his cities, towns and villages, and scatter his enemies. I will make all strife among the rulers of men to cease forever. . . . The people of their lands shall be joyous, and upper and lower classes will blend as smoothly as milk and water. They shall appreciate each other's feelings, join happily in diversions together, and with all compassion and modesty increase the sources of goodness.[7]

As Japan entered the Nara period (708-794) this idyllic model formed the core of state ideology, and was joined with other politically useful Mahāyāna sources including both the *Vimalakīrti Sūtra*, glorifying the spiritual prowess of the laity and court aristocracy, and the *Lotus Sūtra*, stressing the unity of all forms of soteriological action in the "one vehicle" now fused with the authority of the state and symbolizing its concern for the welfare of all the people.

Buddhist sectarian doctrines found institutional expression in newly imported schools representing both Hīnayāna and Mahāyāna teachings, including the Mādhyamika (Sanron) and Vijñānavāda (Hossō).[8] Buddhism dominated the religious life of the royal court and was patronized through the building of temples and monasteries, and in other acts of merit-making piety. It provided important ceremonial media for reinforcing court solidarity and satisfying the aesthetic interests of the aristocracy.

The philosophical subtleties of the scholastic commentaries could have been comprehended only by a small minority. But some of the early Nara schools—particularly the Kegon (Hua-yen) centered around the *Avataṃsaka Sūtra*—were inherently congenial to the needs of the state: the emperor was identified with *Lochana* (Vairocana) Buddha, and the larger society with his phenomenal emanations, all mutually interdependent and "not impeding each other." In 741 the emperor Shōmu ordered copies of the *Golden Light Sūtra* sent to all the provinces. He directed the building of provincial temples staffed with suitable personnel and built a central shrine housing an immense statue of the Lochana Buddha.[9]

By the mid-eighth century, Buddhism was the cultic and ideological center of the state; and the Saṅgha rose to a position of unprecedented economic and political power. Although the rigorous provisions of the monastic rule formed the special discipline of one of the Nara schools, the Jōjitsu, this did not abate worldly compromises and accommodations. The most striking example of this problem was the attempt of a master of the Hossō school to assume the throne. Hossō had a special appeal for some members of the aristocracy, since one of its fundamental doctrines was that the essential Buddha-nature was *not* inherent in all human beings; enlightenment could be attained only by a select few, a special spiritual elite. Shōmu's daughter, the empress Shōtoku, actually proposed to abdicate the throne in favor of the Hossō monk Dōkyō whom she had already appointed chief minister of state.[10] His monastic vows did not impair his political ambitions. This potential Caesaro-papist theocracy was finally blocked by opposing forces in the royal court. At the close of the Nara and the beginning of the Heian period (794-1191) the Buddhist clergy was significantly discredited because of its hand in these political upheavals and apparent abrogation of moral and ascetic standards.

The new emperor, Kammu, deliberately undertook to dissociate the court from the Nara schools by moving the capital bodily to Kyoto and coining the term *Heian* ("peace," "tranquillity") to express his new political and cultural goals. He also encouraged the formation of a new

Buddhist monastic order on nearby Mount Hiei under the leadership of Saichō (767-822), a reforming monk of Chinese lineage who had earlier withdrawn in disgust from the worldly meshes of Nara Buddhism.

Saichō established his own spiritual and doctrinal independence by studying with T'ien-t'ai (Tendai) monks in China. He centered his teaching around the *Lotus Sūtra*, stressing its universal relevance to all men, and the necessity for moral rigor. He asserted that "all human beings have the lotus of Buddhahood within them. It will rise above the mire and foul water of the Hīnayāna and pseudo-Mahāyāna [the Nara schools] . . . in full glory."[11] His monks, many of whom came from China and Korea, were required to undergo twelve years of study and discipline under the rules of the Vinaya. His specific social aim was to prepare them to assume positions of responsible leadership in joint support of the monastic order and the state as teachers, administrators, and even engineering technicians for "the repair of ponds and canals, construction of bridges and ships, digging of wells and irrigation ditches." The monastic center was designated "Chief Seat of the Buddhist Religion for Ensuring the Protection of the Country" and was tied rigidly to the authority of the patrimonial court. Upon entry the monks were required to take an oath of allegiance to "the Three Treasures (and) the saintly Emperor Kammu on behalf of Japan." Lay supervisors with direct coercive powers were set up "to keep out robbers, liquor, and women." Saichō's model of kingship and social ethics is distinctly Confucian:

His majesty the Emperor is equal to the sun and the moon in enlightenment, and his virtue does not differ from that of heaven and earth. His administration is in accord with the five human relationships, and his religious faith is based on the teachings of Buddha.[12]

State sponsorship promoted the steady growth of Tendai, and the complex on Mount Hiei was an immense establishment in its heyday, with 3,000 buildings and 30,000 monks. But even in Saichō's era its privileged status provoked bitter hostility, particularly from the Nara schools.

This problem was compounded with Kammu's death in A.D. 806. The new emperor asserted his own patrimonial independence by promoting a new teaching expounded by Kūkai (Kōbō Daishi, 774-835), a monk of aristocratic lineage who had studied in China and returned with a rich repertoire of Tantric Buddhist teachings culled from the Chen-yen ("True-word") school. With the emperor's support, Kūkai—a man unquestionably of immense intellectual and artistic abilities—founded Shingon, the Japanese version of this school, and he built a monastery on Mount Koya in deliberate antithesis to Saichō's Tendai on Mount Hiei.

The esoteric teachings of Shingon, rich in ceremonials and aesthetically satisfying symbolism, appealed to the royal court. Shingon claimed to incorporate not only all the major Buddhist doctrines, but Confucianism, Taoism and Brāhmanism as well, forming a hierarchical system capped by the esoteric mysteries and gilded by the graphic and plastic arts. As outlined in Kūkai's *Ten Stages of Religious Consciousness*, it provided an eclectic system of beliefs and practices capable of wide-ranging social penetration which could be accommodated to the given social hierarchy through extension of the highest esoteric privileges to the elite. The maṇḍalas, the mudrās, the mantras —the visual and aural ornamentation, music, incense, ceremonial pageantry, and magical spells—were all integrated with his pedagogy.

Kūkai's theory of Buddhist aesthetics is formally stated,

and reflects a profound insight into the problem of religious symbolism in general.

The Dharma has no speech, but without speech it cannot be communicated. Highest truth transcends color, but only by means of color can it be understood. Mistakes will be made in the effort to point at truth, for there is no clearly defined method of teaching, but even when art does not excite admiration . . . it is a treasure which protects the country and benefits the people. . . . [Its source] is Buddha's love. . . . Art is what reveals to us the state of perfection.[13]

Shingon's synthetic potential also found one of its most important expressions in Dual (Ryōbu) Shintō, in which Shintō gods were designated bodhisattvas in an effort to form a unified cultic framework. The pre-eminence of Buddhism, here, lies in the fact that the Shintō gods were regarded as particular worldly manifestations of the higher and more generalized principle of bodhisattva spirituality.

Saichō's relations with Kūkai were at first cordial, and the Tendai master actually studied extensively with Kūkai. But when the latter insisted on Saichō's submission to Shingon superiority a permanent and bitter rift developed. This conflict was exacerbated when, after Saichō's death Kūkai was appointed chief priest of the royal temple and had the audacity to place Tendai doctrine below Shingon and Kegon in his Ten Stages hierarchy.

The obvious syncretic power and popularity of Shingon moved Saichō's successor Ennin (794-864) to institute a full-blown Tendai esotericism based on his own studies in China. Tendai finally surpassed Shingon in prestige, partly because of its proximity to the royal capital. But Tendai itself was victimized by a sectarian disruption stemming from a dispute over the right of patriarchal succession which developed when the emperor selected a blood relative of the aristocratic Kūkai as abbot of one of the most important Tendai temples.

This conflict developed into one of the most tragic periods in the history of Japanese Buddhism. The two camps not only split into hostile religious "sects" but, in coordination with dominant clan-based feudal developments, formed fortresses of warrior-monks engaged in violent internecine warfare. During the medieval period this became a widespread sectarian characteristic. These hostilities were exacerbated by the fact that personal status depended on education in one of the monasteries and its respective position vis-à-vis royal or clan approval. Centralized imperial control, always tenuous at best, slowly gave way to centrifugal provincial loyalties. Clan conflict was frequently defined along "religious" lines with the great families supporting one feudal monastery against another. Equally important was the free-wheeling legitimation allowed by the syncretic richness of the esoteric teachings. It provided the symbolic media for almost any kind of rationalization, including suitable Shintō warrior deities to signify the solidarity of each monastic fortress.[14]

This dissolution of social and symbolic control is also evident in the fact that the esoteric milieu easily accommodated magical cults devoted to techniques for the prolongation of life or the gaining of special worldly ends; and it also found expression in the Vajrayāna sexual-sacramentalism of the Tachikawa school, a "heretical" movement bitterly opposed by Shingon leaders and ultimately suppressed by imperial order.

From the viewpoint of the state there were also new possibilities for royal legitimation: in the ninth century Emperor Uda instituted the practice of abdicating the throne ostensibly in favor of the monastic life, while actually controlling a boy "emperor" from within the sanctuary of the Saṅgha—a remarkable fusion of theocratic and divine kingship (tennō) concepts.

In all of this, the resurgent Buddhism of the early Heian seemed to have undergone another compromising worldly domestication. However, towards the end of the Heian period, amid increasingly violent clan wars and social disruptions, there were countervailing forces at work. In the late Heian court, clearly under the influence of Buddhism, we find the emergence of a self-reflective poetry, literature, and drama—most notably expressed in the *Tales of Genji*—marked by an extraordinary sophistication of mood and expression. Awareness of the transience of life and the melancholy of impermanent beauty were aesthetically important experiences. This was coupled with symbolism of withdrawal, a nostalgia for the tranquillity of the past (*sabi*), and an inarticulate need for incorruptible transcendence (*yūgen*). While it is true that this easily degenerated into sentimentality and became a sign of courtly refinement (*miyabi*) which reinforced aristocratic solidarity, it nevertheless signifies a growing uneasiness, and a renewed sense of human finitude, transience, and guilt; and it developed into powerful art forms during the next centuries.[15]

The increasingly violent feudal wars finally resulted in the overthrow of the old Kyoto aristocracy and the installation of military rule under the Kamakura Shogunate (1192-1333). However, effective political stabilization did not take place until the Tokugawa period, and during the intervening four centuries Japan was continually devastated by protracted warfare. In this situation of deepening gloom and pessimism, the energies of Buddhism were once again restored in a breakthrough which touched all levels of society. The feeling of despair and powerlessness transcended class distinctions. There was a shift in the balance of power from the capital to the provinces dominated by a new class of landowners and warriors (the *Samurai*);[16] and thus liberated from its aristocratic embeddedness in the defunct Kyoto court, Buddhist universalism took several new directions expressed in ways which still characterize Japanese religious life today.

The most important single expression of this new universalism was Pure Land Buddhism. The message was basically the same as in the Chinese case: in this age of utter decay and corruption self-salvation is impossible. Only Amitābha's (Amida's) grace suffices. The single efficacious act is the fervent invocation and repetition of Amida's name: the *nembutsu* (*namu Amida butsu*). This practice had already been introduced to Japan by Ennin, Tendai's master of esoteric teaching. Originally it signified meditation on Amida's name, and only secondarily prayerful invocation. But even the name-repetition itself later came to be regarded as a sign of "self-power"—an ironic affirmation of man's finitude and helplessness.[17]

The most striking institutional features of the movement were, first, its egalitarian social grounding: the "democracy" of despair meant that religious solace and solidarity would inevitably find expression in a more inclusive network of commonly held values which cut through traditional class divisions; second, the dissolution of ascriptive ecclesiastical barriers: celibate monastic self-perfection, the exclusion of women, esotericism, and clerical aristocracies were all subject to massive corrosion; third, the emergence of a new religious elite whose status was based on power to communicate Amida's presence at popular levels through symbols expressing personal devotion, faith, love, and the certainty of salvation.

Pure Land was first promoted during the late Heian period by three unorthodox Tendai priests who broke

through monastic barriers to answer a deep-felt calling:
Kūya (903-972), Genshin (942-1017), and Ryōnin (1072-
1132). Kūya left the monastery to promote his devotion
to Amida among the masses. He danced and sang in the
streets, leading his loosely formed congregations in song.
He engaged in public works, building bridges and digging
wells, and his missionary zeal even moved him to try to
evangelize the primitive Ainus. Genshin, who remained
in the monastic order, popularized Amidism in his book
The Essentials of Salvation, a selection of passages from
a wide range of Buddhist scriptures designed to illustrate
the basic principles of the faith. It reflects the ethos of the
times and the special values of Pure Land:

The teaching and practice which leads to birth in Paradise is
the most important thing in this impure world during these
degenerate times. Monks and Laymen, men of high or low station, who will not turn to it? But the teachings of the Buddha
are not in one text . . . and they are very complex. . . . How
could a stupid person like me ever attain such knowledge?
Therefore I have chosen the one gate to salvation . . . the
Nembutsu.[18]

The book develops an elaborate heaven-hell cosmology,
and dwells on the torments awaiting those who kill living
creatures—an expression of revulsion against the murderous holocausts of the era. Genshin treated the same
subjects in painting and scripture, with powerful effect
according to the tradition, establishing the visual arts as
a new medium for popular instruction. Ryōnin popularized
the teaching through music and liturgy, chanting the
nembutsu and urging the unity of all men with imagery
drawn from Tendai and Kegon teaching: "one in all and
all in one," mankind and Amida share each other in faith.
His converts included monks, aristocrats, and common laity
alike. Subsequent developments were even more radical.

Ippen (1239-1289) followed the tradition of personal
evangelism, preaching and singing about the omnipresence
of Amida's compassion and grace in Shintō shrines and
Buddhist temples with a universalism which transcended
all sectarian differences. His *Precepts* are an epitome of
these new values and of traditional Buddhist morality:

> Devoutly practice the invocation;
> Do not engage in superfluous disciplines.
> Devoutly trust the law of love;
> Do not denounce the creeds of others.
> Devoutly promote the sense of equality;
> Do not arouse discriminatory feelings.
> Devoutly awaken the sense of compassion;
> Do not forget the sufferings of others.
> Devoutly examine your own faults. . . .
> Beware of lust, greed, and anger.[19]

The sudden increase in the popularity of Pure Land
during this period of hardship suggests that for the first
time the meaning of the human situation—not merely the
immediate conditions of personal well-being—was called
into question on a large scale. There was an increasing
obsession with the idea that the world is hell and the
human situation totally corrupt. It is true that for many
the heavenly rewards were an affirmation of this world's
unattainable pleasures, and the aristocracy brought Pure
Land symbolism into court life through decorous ceremony
and art, but there were other practices symptomatic of
deeper stresses: people of all classes practiced ascetic vigils
and fasts while concentrating on Amida's compassionate
image. There were radical acts of physical self-mortification, the gift of a finger, hand, or arm to Amida; religious
suicides by burning or drowning. All were indicative of
profound disturbance.

Hōnen (1133-1212) and his disciple Shinran (1173-
1262) were responsible for the major forms of Pure Land

which still exist today. They both studied Tendai, and were—despite their claims to the contrary—immensely learned. But the ritual and scholastic labyrinth did not lead to enlightenment. They felt as ignorant and as helpless as many others outside the monastery.

Prior to Hōnen's efforts, the images of Amida were to be found in the temples of almost every sect, and the nembutsu had no orthodox exclusiveness. But Hōnen insisted on the inherent superiority of Amidism over all other religious practices, and stressed the uselessness of all other doctrines of salvation. For Hōnen only one thing is necessary: complete commitment to Amida and faithful invocation of his name; all other acts are superfluous. His radical sectarianism and his success in winning converts culminated in persecution and final exile.

Hōnen's formal justification for this dogmatic stance was based on the old theory of the "easy path": the human situation is so corrupt that monastic striving is useless, but this was reinforced by his conviction that the Buddha himself propounded it as his highest teaching: "the very thing that Śākya [the Buddha] himself entrusted to his disciple Ānanda." His stress on the unique efficacy of Amida's power comes from the conviction that it was not merely a supplement to other doctrines but qualitatively superior to them within the sacred economy of the final age of degeneration that reduced all men to a condition of sinfulness and ignorance:

Final salvation . . . is nothing but the mere repetition of Amida's name without a doubt of his mercy. . . . Those who believe this, though they understand all the teachings of [the Buddha] should behave like unlettered and ignorant people . . . whose faith is implicitly simple.[20]

Hōnen's disciple Shinran went even further: man's total sinfulness means that calling on Amida's name is a useless effort at merit-making unless it is done out of prior grace-given faith and gratitude. Even more than this, suffering and sin are now the very preconditions for personal salvation: "if the good are saved how much more the wicked." Since it is faith alone that counts, all traditional norms are abrogated. Monastic celibacy and the Vinaya are ineffectual and must be abandoned. The warrior, hunter, thief, murderer, prostitute—all are saved through faith.

His logic is clear: in the face of Amida's power and grace it is truly blasphemous and pathetically errant to suppose that one's own conduct, virtue, or life situation can have any effect on spiritual status. Furthermore, Amida's power of redemption is particularly and dramatically attested where it is manifest among the ignorant, the outcast, and the sinful:

Amida's Holy Name is the power that determines our entrance into his Pure Land. . . . If once there be aroused in us but one thought of joy and love, we turn first as we are with our sins and lusts upon us, towards Nirvana.[21]

Ethical behavior is a free expression of gratitude and love.

Shinran did not found a separate sect. It developed at first informally in reaction to some of the more conservative elements in Hōnen's group who still held to the ideal of monastic celibacy and other traditional vows. Shinran had married and raised a family, not because he regarded marriage as an expression of personal freedom from the traditional monastic vows, but because celibacy was a form of "self-power" and an expression of inadequate faith in Amida's grace. The new sect—"True Pure Land" (Jōdo Shin)—was later organized by Shinran's lineal descendants in a patriarchy of blood charisma.

One of the most important consequences of Pure Land radicalism was that it provoked a counter-reformation which brought new rigor to the Nara sects and reform movements within Shingon and Tendai. The most important reformer was Nichiren (1222-1282)—a Tendai monk born the son of a fisherman who took pride in his lowly birth and messianic calling.[22] His reforming message was based on a call to return to the pure teaching of the *Lotus Sūtra* expressed through repetition of the name of the sūtra alone. The goal of his mission was a paradoxical combination of evangelical universalism, radical sectarianism, and fierce nationalism, demanding the cultural and political unification of Japan around Buddhism through faith in the *Lotus*. His messianic role and authority were clear to him:

The Lord Shākya proclaimed [in the *Lotus Sūtra*] that when all the truths of Buddhism should be shrouded in darkness, the Bodhisattva of Superb Action should be commissioned to save the most wicked of men. . . . Those who propagate the Lotus of Truth are indeed the parents of all living in Japan. . . . I, Nichiren, am the master and lord of the sovereign as well as of all the Buddhists of other schools.[23]

He particularly despised Hōnen and the Pure Land for reasons which reveal his concern for institutional authority and coherence:

Woe, woe!
    From princes and barons down to the common people, everyone is saying that there are no Scriptures. . . . As a consequence of [Hōnen's] preaching, men refused to make contributions to temples that were not dedicated to Amida and forgot to pay their tithes to priests . . . , and so the priests and deities who protected the people have left the temples and refuse to return. . . .[24]

His position was so radical that he formed a new school which provoked bitter hostility, and his criticism of the incumbent regime for failure to heed his warnings resulted in the imposition of a death sentence finally commuted to exile. His suffering he interpreted not only as inherently in keeping with the Buddha's message, but as a sign of his own calling ("Every place where Nichiren encounters perils is the Buddha's land"). Moral standards were vigorously upheld, in part through the karmic theodicy which he applied unstintingly to himself: "That Nichiren suffers so much is not without remote causes. . . . who, indeed fully knows the sins accumulated in his previous lives? . . . The accumulated karma is unfathomable."[25] His disciples continued missionary activity under continuous persecution, particularly during the Tokugawa Shogunate. The atmosphere of pugnacious spirituality, physical courage, and aggressive self-certainty were appealing models which gained and held the respect of many followers and admirers through subsequent centuries, though Nichiren's school did not approach the popularity of Pure Land.

Zen Buddhism was the third major movement to emerge out of the Kamakura matrix, though it did not reach full strength until the Ashikaga Shogunate (1333-1572) and after. Its soteriology was the reverse of the Pure Land and Nichiren sects, and it did not find equally popular social grounding. But for the reasons noted above it was immensely appealing to many individuals for whom neither otherworldly cosmologies nor martyrdom were meaningful forms of religious action. It did, however, have several things in common with the Pure Land and Nichiren schools: a simplified spiritual goal and techniques stressing immediacy, personal relevance, and practical consequences —all within the range of ordinary men.

Zen was successfully transplanted to Japan by two key figures. Eisai (1141-1215) and Dōgen (1200-1253). Dissatisfied with the condition of Tendai Buddhism, Eisai left for Sung China where he studied with a Lin-chi (Rinzai) master. After returning to Japan he settled in Kamakura where his eminently practical teaching found popular acceptance among the new warrior aristocracy. Later he went to Kyoto with the intention of blending both Shingon and Tendai esotericism with his doctrine. His alliance with the new political order and his compromise with the other sects were major factors in the successful institutionalization of Zen in Japan. He felt obliged to justify Zen as conducive to national welfare. In a tract entitled *The Propagation of Zen for the Protection of the Country* he argues that Zen "propagates the Truth as the Buddha did, with the robe of authentic transmission from one man to the next." He denies that it is "nihilist" and asserts that it is "the key to all forms of Buddhism . . . the Highest Inner Wisdom." The monastic ethic, celibacy, and mendicancy were staunchly upheld.[26]

Dōgen, a Tendai monk of aristocratic birth, first studied with Eisai's disciples and then went to China to study with a master of the "gradualist" Ts'ao-tung (Sōtō) school. He tried to strike a balance between the patriarchal and scriptural traditions, approving both Hīnayāna and Mahāyāna sources and minimizing the idea that enlightenment is a sudden and final experience: his teaching stressed rational modes of self-perfection through meditation, and ethical and intellectual striving:

Enlightenment may seem to come to an end, but though it appears to have stopped, it should be prolonged. . . . The main thing is to pass the time sitting upright without any thought of reward or attaining enlightenment. . . . By reflecting only on the kōan and the dialogues of the patriarchs one may be led astray from the way of the Buddha. . . . To discard the sutras of the Buddha is to reject the mind of the Buddha . . . and when you have abandoned the teaching . . . what will be left except a lot of bald-headed monks? . . . Then you would certainly deserve to be enslaved by the rulers of this world![27]

Dōgen retained a strong sense of the dignity of the mendicant life, physical labor, and discipline, rejecting an easy accommodation of moral rigor to given conditions.

Some say that the propagation of Buddhism in these latter degenerate days would be enhanced if the monks had no worries over food, clothing, and the like; but such a place would only attract the selfish and worldly. . . .[28]

Though he refused to lend open support to the incumbent political regime, Zen teaching in general provided a remarkably creative base for coordination with the secular needs and cultural goals of the state. Zen monks assisted the emperor in many tasks, helping to cement diplomatic and economic relations with China as business managers and entrepreneurs. They were instrumental in establishing a state-sponsored Buddhist church during the Ashikaga Shogunate which included the importation and promulgation of Sung Neo-Confucianism, educational services, and the printing of textbooks.[29] Equally important was the liberalizing influence of Zen on the arts, from painting and flower arrangement to archery and swordsmanship (utility and grace, discipline, selflessness, and spontaneity), and many aesthetic refinements which became part of the mainstream of Japanese cultural life.

The egalitarian thrust of these new religious movements which were initiated during the Kamakura period contributed richly to the religious and cultural vitality of Japanese society, but they were not basically "social-reforming." Though there was much criticism of particular political leaders, it did not undercut feudal or patrimonial institutions. Although at first these movements broke through the social boundaries of the old aristocracy, they often supported the ethic of the new warrior class in many direct and indirect ways by reinforcing the feudal leader-follower nexus. The demand for unswerving loyalty to the lord had structural and psychological parallels with the authority of the Zen master, and the True Pure Land hereditary patriarch. The early prophetic tension was also syphoned off in other ways: through the aesthetic life which Zen promoted so richly by affirming the inner spiritual validity of the natural world as it is given, or in the otherworldly piety of the Pure Land devotee which did not give rise to rational social criticism but, rather, to discrete philanthropies or violent expressions of group solidarity. In the late medieval period Shinran's True Pure Land sect—centered around the hereditary patriarchate—developed into a militant feudal organization with vested political and economic interests.[30] Zen values were integrated with the warrior code (*Bushidō*). Its mystical affirmation of the world tended to support an uncritical acceptance of social and political institutions, and the manipulation of the personality for more "efficient" fulfillment of given political roles. At the popular level it easily assimilated magical techniques and liturgies remote from the tradition of the masters.

As the rationalization of state Shintō and the first glimmerings of a real national ideology began to emerge, Buddhism was increasingly regarded as a political menace precisely because it gravitated toward clan particularism and, with the exception of Zen, seemed to add little to political or economic reason. In 1571 the military unification of Japan by General Oda Nobunaga was dramatized by the deliberate destruction of the Tendai establishments, including the razing of the temple complex on Mount Hiei and the massacre of many of its inhabitants. He also besieged and finally conquered the True Pure Land sanctuaries. His pretext was that they had provided refuge for political rebels; but the more general reason given was that they obstructed "the maintenance of law and order in the country," a notion which presaged subsequent events affecting the fate of Buddhism in Japan during the next two centuries.[31]

5. *Aspects of the Contemporary Situation*

THE ADVENT of European colonialism and the diffusion of Western values and institutions throughout Asia precipitated far-reaching strains and innovations. The major modernizing pressures took the form of resurgent nationalism, democratic aspirations, the development of rational science and industrialization, including, inevitably, the corrosive acids of the secular ideologies—all of which placed new demands on the Sangha for critical self-reflection and reform.

Characteristically, throughout Theravādin lands the Buddha is now often represented as the first modern "psychologist" and "scientist," concerned with the analytical understanding of the human situation and the need for innovation and progress.[1] The monastic leadership was placed under new pressures to justify the immense drain on the economy which state support of the Sangha represented and to bridge the gap between its traditional values and the modernizing goals of the state. The principles of love and noninjury are often regarded as basic axioms for organized social action and reform, particularly in the new Buddhist youth movements and missionary societies. The value of the merit-making metaphysic has been refocused on the need for supporting national ideology and new economic and technological goals.

The Saṅgha also sees itself as a harbinger of international peace, apparently unattainable in the West, and as a bulwark against the erosions of Western secularism and materialism. For the fifth Theravādin council, in 1871, the canonical scriptures were inscribed in stone partly to symbolize the permanency of the teaching in the face of dehumanizing Western values. At the assembly of the sixth council, in Rangoon, Burma, in 1954-1956, there was a new stress on the international solidarity of all Buddhists with respect to the constructive missionary goals of Buddhism in the modern world.[2]

The Western-educated laity and certain members of the monastic elite have been the most influential factors in bringing about internal reforms. When constitutional monarchies and the franchise were introduced they undermined the traditional relationship between the monastic order and the old aristocracy. Many of the new reforming movements were initiated by nationals in the civil service who had worked for the British and French bureaucracies.

In India, Theravāda Buddhism has returned, partly under government sponsorship of a general program of cultural restoration; and King Aśoka's ethical universalism is a key symbol of India's new national self-awareness. One of the most notable social contributions which Buddhism has made in India is its emergence under the leadership of the late B. R. Ambedkar (1891-1957) as a political protest movement against caste discrimination. His case is a particularly striking example of the selective use of traditional Buddhist values under the guidance of Western humanistic rationalism and political goals.[3]

Ambedkar was a member of the Mahars—one of the largest and most depressed untouchable castes, traditionally relegated to demeaning tasks of village sanitation and menial labor. In the early twentieth century several Mahar leaders made limited efforts to develop communal solidarity and obtain some relief through mild protest movements and appeals to the British crown. Ambedkar's advantage over his predecessors was his ambition and opportunity for a thorough education in the Western style. Significantly, he was from an army family, one of only two high school graduates from among the Mahars, and he obtained a scholarship to study in England and America. In 1917 he received his Ph.D. from Columbia University; and upon his return to India immediately became a public spokesman for the cause of the Untouchables. His 1919 testimony before the Bombay Presidency reveals the power of his natural and acquired intellectual resources: "Socioreligious disabilities have dehumanized the untouchable. . . . [They] are so socialized as never to complain of their low estate. . . ."[4]

He was not at first interested in religious issues, except negatively, insofar as Hinduism reinforced social barriers; and he urged the depressed castes to concentrate on secular education, self-improvement, and independent political action. This brought him into conflict with Gandhi, who insisted on a policy of religious reform within the framework of Hindu culture and institutions. Gandhi's intransigence finally turned Ambedkar to overt criticism of Hinduism *in toto*, since he viewed it as basically intractable.[5] He resolved that he would "not die in the Hindu religion," and began to look openly for non-Hindu religious alternatives—at first to Islam, Christianity, and Sikhism— while continuing to promote secular political action. His decision not to convert was partly due to his knowledge

that mass conversion would deprive his people of govern-
ment-sponsored reparations and privileges extended only
to the specifically Hindu depressed castes.[6] It is interesting
to note that at no time did he consider Communism a
viable alternative. He regarded it as an elitist ideology led
by a "bunch of Brāhman boys." The violence of Marxist
political history was also abhorrent to him; and he recognized its inherent lack of rapport with the radically dis-
privileged, and the near primitive conditions and men-
tality of outcaste life.

The war years intervened, and official independence in
1947 found him in Nehru's cabinet as law minister. But
he resigned this position in 1951 chiefly because of the
cabinet's unwillingness to support his demands for wide-
ranging and immediate reforms. His search for ways to
effect large-scale social change turned him once again to
religion. His interest in the Buddha and Buddhism was
actually of long standing, but its institutional weakness
in India appeared, at first, to be a disadvantage. However,
in 1948 he had advanced the somewhat mythologized
thesis that the Untouchables had originally been Buddhists
reduced to outcaste status by orthodox Brāhmanism. In
1951 he wrote *The Buddha and His Dhamma* in which
the classical anticaste critique and rational social values
of the teaching were underscored; and he began to consider the possibility of mass conversion. On October 14,
1956, four months before his death, he formally converted
to the Buddhist faith at the hands of the oldest Buddhist
monk in India along with about 500,000 of his followers.[7]
Shortly after his conversion he addressed a meeting of the
World Fellowship of Buddhists on "Buddha and Karl
Marx," observing that Buddhist social teachings were
rigorously egalitarian and embued with a doctrine of love
and spirituality unknown to the Marxists. The retention of

a specifically Indian value system was important to him, since it meshed with strongly defined cultural and national sensibilities while at the same time undercutting Hindu sanctions.

The new "Buddhist" Mahars in many village quarters joyfully and often unceremoniously removed the Hindu deities from their houses, and in many instances refused to perform the menial tasks which Hindu tradition required of them. This new sense of liberated solidarity was combined with pressures for internal communal reforms, especially in accordance with the five lay precepts, to raise the customary morals and debased life-style of the community. There was also a deepening interest in Buddhist religious culture *per se*: rites, ceremonies, and devotional life. And Ambedkar himself was soon a revered saint second only to the Buddha.

However, in all of this, the immense burden of India's economic and political problems seem overpowering. "Buddhist" is often an epithet for "untouchable" in Maharashtra, and is regarded by upwardly mobile groups within the community as an embarrassing link to its still backward members.[8] As elsewhere, the political viability of Buddhism in India is still under test.

In Indochina, to take the Thai case once again, an initial positive response by the royal house to French colonialism and Catholicism was followed by a conservative reaction approved by the Saṅgha, resulting in the usurpation of the throne. The fear of political and economic domination was directly tied to the fear of a loss of religious identity: "The foreigners . . . will attack this kingdom on every side, and the Buddhist religion will decline and fall into dishonor."[9] The Theravādin base of Thai national independence remained relatively stable and well defined; but where colonial forces triumphed, as in Burma and Ceylon, the situation was quite different. Burmese resistance to British military advances was at first strongly reinforced by the Saṅgha and the royal court: "The English barbarians (will) destroy our religion, violate our national customs and degrade our race. . . ."[10] But when the colonial government gained final political control, it cut the crucial lines of traditional authority between state and Saṅgha by displacing the royal house and refusing to enforce the decisions of the Buddhist primate on the grounds that this would abrogate the principle of religious neutrality and freedom. The result was the undermining of the primary means of religious legitimation and social control from the central government down to the village level, with consequent internal disorders in the Saṅgha and the massive disaffection of its leadership. This was exacerbated by Christian missionizing and the introduction of secular colonial courts and education. Nationalist counteroffensives were mounted at a number of levels, all imbued with Buddhist values: In 1906 Burma's Young Men's Buddhist Association was formed by members of the small Western-educated middle class who deliberately appropriated the model of the Christian voluntary association first developed in Ceylon (1890) to muster anti-British sentiments and promote indigenous cultural values through rational techniques.

The disintegrated monastic orders produced new politically oriented leaders, most notably represented by the monk U Ottama (d. 1939), who had studied Gandhi's techniques first hand in India: "[Monks] pray for nibbāna but slaves can never attain it, therefore they must pray for release from slavery in this life";[11] and he urged programs of passive resistance by Hindus, Muslims, and Buddhists alike. These techniques were supplemented with acts of open rebellion often led by extremist monks with grass-roots shamanistic appeal at the village level.[12] Widespread disorders in the late thirties degenerated into religious riots between Buddhists and Muslims, and a soaring crime rate.

In all of this the role played by Buddhism at the most general level was to provide the most widely shared symbols for the expression of a vast range of grievances; it was the only medium for the shaping of an anticolonial ideology. The problems of internal order in the Saṅgha, secular parliamentary government, and the corrosion of traditional beliefs received scant attention. However, after independence these issues were and still are manifest in many ways, perhaps most strikingly in the political activities of premier U Nu who dominated the scene from 1948 to 1962. Elected in 1948, U Nu undertook to reintegrate Burma through a synthesis of traditional Buddhist, democratic, and socialist institutions. Although his commitment to Buddhism appeared to be politically appropriate, in fact, his personal piety was irrationally profound, and seems in retrospect to have been the source of his undoing.[13] At the outset his activities seemed canny and highly reasonable: with few exceptions Buddhism was the single link that traditionally united the various provincial ethnic groups—Burmans, Shans, Mons, and Arakanese—and also linked the various classes from the illiterate masses to the educated elite. The extreme secular nationalists and even the Marxists were obliged to demonstrate appropriate piety for popular support. Furthermore, it would seem that the rational content of Buddhist teaching could easily be manipulated to accommodate "socialist" economics, democratic institutions, and science. Under his leadership Parliament instituted the Ecclesiastical Courts Acts in 1949 and 1951 to strengthen the internal organization of the Saṅgha. The Pāli University and Education Board Acts

(1950, 1952) restored the tradition of Pāli Scholarship, examinations, and rewards. The Buddha Sāsana Act (1950) designated a board of laymen responsible for promoting Buddhism in coordination with the Saṅgha. At vast national expense he sponsored the Sixth Buddhist Council held in Rangoon from 1954 to 1956; and in 1961 largely through his efforts Buddhism was named the official state religion. All of this was immensely important to the general resurgence of Buddhist culture and in promoting international solidarity with respect to Buddhist missionary goals. Its productive achievements and long-range consequences have yet to be measured.

However, **against** this background it also appears in retrospect, first, that the immensely intractable problems of modern social and economic organization in Burma could not be resolved through a resurgence of traditional Buddhist culture or managed through apparent rational analogues; second, that the status of Buddhism as a state religion meant the inevitable alienation of religious minorities and the secularists; and third, that the premier's increasing personal preoccupation with devotional practices often bordering on magic, which he intended to serve as a model of individual piety for each citizen, was often a substitute for structured socioeconomic and political policies and reforms. Characteristically, in 1951 U Nu stated that Burma's social problems were the result of religious apathy. Parliament must encourage every individual to root out greed (*lobha*), delusion (*moha*), and hatred (*dosa*). Black-marketeering and other disruptive business practices were contrary to the doctrine of love (mettā); the supreme goal of economic and political viability is to provide leisure and freedom so that all may strive for the attainment of salvation. The immoral struggle for acquisition of worldly goods is a fatal flaw inherent in the capitalist system. He also spent much effort to prove that Marxism and Buddhism were inherently compatible,[14] but reversed this position when the Marxists proved to be increasingly critical: ("The wisdom or knowledge that might be attributed to Karl Marx is less than one-tenth of a particle of dust that lies at the feet of Lord Buddha"); Marxist materialism is incompatible with the doctrines of anattā and anicca, as are its authoritarian and violent methods.

His nonauthoritarian mood, deeply imbued with the doctrine of ahiṃsā ("I fear saṃsāra"), undercut the executive rigor necessary to implement the various ecclesiastical reform bills. Members of the Saṅgha stoutly resisted efforts to regulate the order so that it could provide a stable bureaucratic base for social reconstruction. In this respect the old monarchial system had a somewhat ironic advantage over the democratic model, in that it was the responsibility of the royal autocrat to "cleanse the Saṅgha" by force if necessary as the "defender of the faith." The Thai regime retained much of this traditional concept of authority; the Thai Saṅgha, twice the size of its Burmese counterpart, was carefully regulated, including ID cards and rigorously enforced hierarchical supervision to prevent drones, moral reprobates, and politically inspired adventurers from gaining institutional controls. "Modernization" in Thailand was carried on first by the royal house and later by the secular government with a relatively large measure of stability due in part to the fact that colonial disruptions were successfully resisted or minimized. Western political institutions, and bureaucratic and educational reforms have been used to reinforce the central role of the Thai Saṅgha as the cultural and religious arm of the state. These innovations were effected chiefly by pressures from the royal house, including the sponsorship

of sectarian movements within the Saṅgha which liberal-
ized traditional values.[15] The tragic paradox in the Burmese case is that the moral superiority, spirituality, and
genuinely exalted ethic of U Nu's Buddhist pietism and
democratic commitments made enforced change impossible.

Even more striking was his fundamentalist adherence
to karmic supernaturalism and his promotion of the primitive symbolism of native traditions. He was an ardent
devotee of the animistic cult of the Nats, for which he
demanded and received government sponsorship—in part
doubtless to retain religious rapport with the masses, but
also quite clearly in the belief that prayer, propitiation,
and good karma had real merit-making power to sustain
the state through its many difficulties. Related irrationalities appeared: the doctrine of ahiṃsā had led to the
prohibition of beef-eating—an immense irritant to the
Muslims and other minorities; and the generally septic
conditions of urban life were exacerbated by government
disinterest in programs to eliminate insects and rodent
vermin, including thousands of stray dogs and other rabies-
carriers. U Nu's piety was often most in evidence where
problems of structured economic and political change were
most pressing. In November, 1961, at his request, the
ministry of religious affairs directed the simultaneous construction at an astrologically auspicious moment of 60,000
sand pagodas throughout Burma "to avert impending
dangers . . . ." It is possible to argue that this was a
thoroughly rational act, given the predominance of the
magical world-view among the masses and in the face of
insuperable economic and political problems. The symbolic reinforcement of a feeling of value solidarity in this
form is not without rational "merit." But it also smacked
of helpless obscurantism and megalomania. The sarcastic

editorial comments from some members of the press reflected an increasingly overt dissatisfaction with these trends. Many educated Buddhists regarded Nat worship and supernaturalist merit-making as a panacea for simpletons.

The progressive alienation of religious minorities and the secular elites finally culminated on March 2, 1961, with the military *coup* headed by General Ne Win. U Nu went into exile, and the official status of Buddhism as the state religion was undone. The military regime sought to preserve the socialist format while rejecting Marxist tenets by immersing it in an ideology which stressed vague religious concepts sufficiently generalized to be acceptable to all: "The welfare of man shall be our main concern. The progress of man shall be our aspiration. And the material and spiritual happiness of man shall be the guide in all our activities."[16] Burma has been a closed state since 1961, and it is difficult to assess the present role and status of the Saṅgha. But economic and political problems remain apparently unabated, and the indefatigable U Nu—from his sanctuary in Thailand—has made repeated if highly improbable statements about an incipient return to power. That he is revered by the Saṅgha and large numbers of Burmese cannot be doubted.[17]

Ceylon was never confronted with the large-scale geographical and cultural provincialisms endemic to Indochina, however the problems affecting the role of Buddhism were in certain respects more severe.[18] First, the Westernized middle class was proportionally much larger, better educated, and deeply committed to British liberalism and its institutions. Many were Anglicans or Roman Catholics. When independence came in 1948 this minority was best qualified to assume the responsibility of government, but yet it was increasingly mistrusted by the Buddhists. Second, the Buddhists numbered about 65 percent of the total population. The next largest minority was the Hindu Tamils, who feared a native Buddhist-Sinhalese resurgence; traditional ethnic and religious hatreds ran deep. Third, the monastic orders were split by a unique caste-based sectarianism: the large and powerful Siam sect was drawn exclusively from the old high-caste Goyigāmas. They held traditional feudal estates and temple properties constituting a vast reservoir of wealth, and were both religiously and politically conservative. The Amarapura sect was comprised of monks from castes somewhat lower on the traditional social scale, but still ranking above the Rāmayāna sect which was the only organization open to all without ascriptive preconditions; but it lacked economic and political power.

This anomalous "caste system" within the Buddhist Saṅgha had roots, as we have already noted, in the ancient history of Ceylon.[19] The rationalization of caste and feudal privilege was subtly imbued with the karmic theodicy and hence deeply resistant to innovation. However, in general, the Buddhist majority were at first able to develop a shared ideology directed to the restoration of Buddhism as the official state religion and driven by grievances against real and imagined colonial depredations. The Buddhist revival movement was centered in the All-Ceylon Buddhist Congress, and was expressed in many ways, perhaps most strikingly summarized in a remarkable document *The Betrayal of Buddhism*. The distinctive features of this document are its affirmation of the traditional role of Buddhism in Sinhalese culture as the basis for a united political front, and the assertion that colonial policy and Western materialism—not the endemic problems of internal order and conservatism in the Saṅgha—were the real cause of the debased condition of Buddhism and society in Ceylon. The problems of the obsolescence of the monk and his values, and the transition from a feudal to a modern economy received scant attention:

In a society whose motive force is the acquisition of wealth by fair means or foul, the incidence of violence, crime, drunkenness and gambling is not a matter for surprise. Conversely, when the motive force of society is altered, the attendant evils will diminish and disappear. Till that major revolution in social thinking takes place, only piecemeal and temporary remedies for various particular ills can be suggested. The real and final remedy is the displacement of Western materialistic social and individual values and the establishment of genuine values founded on the Buddha Dhamma.[20]

The secular government under the direction of Prime Minister S. W. Bandaranaike struggled to balance the increasing pressures of the Buddhist majority against the realities of Ceylon's modernizing needs and in the face of complaints by the non-Buddhist minorities. State-sponsored promotion of Buddhism took many forms, including the elevation to university status of two distinguished monastic institutions of higher learning. But this enterprise raised the problem of Western secular education versus traditional sacred studies. Monks who actually obtained a B.A. or M.A. degree might be (and were) tempted to abandon their monastic calling and seek secular positions congruent with their new values. The general nature of this problem is well represented in many formal criticisms leveled by secular observers: "The higher education of the *bhikkhu* [monk] and the higher education of the laity cannot be brought under one organization. . . . Whatever helps the monk [achieve salvation] is of value to him. Judged by this standard it is doubtful that a university education will be of much value."[21] A representative problem in this area was the traditional status of many members of the

Saṅgha as folk-medicine specialists (Ayurvedic medicine), which was especially popular with the rural masses and an important source of monastic authority and income. The Western medical sciences are inherently incompatible with this tradition.

In their unsuccessful efforts to have Buddhism instituted as a state religion, the Buddhist Sinhalese majority provoked bitter opposition from the Tamils, resulting in murderous communal rioting. Government efforts to impose reforms on the Saṅgha—especially those affecting internal authority and traditional temple land holdings—were bitterly resisted. In September, 1959, Bandaranaike was assassinated by a Buddhist monk (also an Ayurvedic physician) who acted on behalf of a conspiracy promoted by a powerful monastic leader whose personal political and economic ambitions had been frustrated by the Bandaranaike regime. One result of this tragic event was the general revulsion of large segments of the population against the Saṅgha, and new pressures for internal reform and purification. However, the end result was in many respects the further hardening of monastic resistance and an increased sense of alienation.

In retrospect, the historical importance of Theravāda Buddhism to the state can be seen to lie in its exoteric ethical teachings, its presumed magical powers to forestall disaster and ensure prosperity, and in the intimate relation of the cult to the rudimentary religious needs of the masses. The doctrine of karmic merit-making always had this fused magico-ethical quality. But where the state lacked the economic and political basis for the emergence of a strong middle class, an inherent factor of instability was introduced, since the royal court was often obliged to "purify" the Saṅgha by force in the absence of a large politically responsible and educated Buddhist laity. The extent to which the structural bifurcation between monk and layman in the Saṅgha and the "otherworldly" orientation of the teaching actually contributed to this problem is difficult to assess. The monastic elite have always been quite capable of worldly commitments to lay social and political needs, but often contemptuous of responsible lay criticism, deeply resistant to change, and, with few exceptions, incapable of taking systematic advantage of the "rational" and "scientific" analogues in the Buddha's teaching— except as defensive apologists.

During the colonial period, where we find new bourgeoisies emerging, their sense of national pride in their Buddhist identity and struggle for independence from colonial rule were paradoxically combined with the assimilation of Western secular values often inimical to the great bulk of traditional Buddhist doctrine, and cultic and magical symbolism. This "value" alienation at the most fundamental level has proved and doubtless will continue to be far more potent than the provisional consensus of national Buddhist sensibilities.

The continued secularization of Theravāda culture touching new monastic recruits and the rural populations on whom the Saṅgha has traditionally depended for much support may be the only long-range solution to these massive problems. This possibility also may mean the final corrosion of the most central values and institutions of traditional Buddhism, a problem shared generally by all of the major religions in the West as well. However, one of the distinctive features of Theravāda Buddhism is the absence of intensive intellectual experimentation and creativity comparable to the theological and philosophical innovations which have been underway among Christian, Jewish, Hindu, and Japanese Buddhist elites. Much of the resurgence of Theravādin Buddhist culture, Pāli scholarship, and communal values has a distinctly formal and traditionalistic quality, and often seems to have been driven mainly by ideological energies. The cultic, magical, and shamanistic underground is regarded as theoretically nonessential. But the ancient metaphysic, the doctrine of karma, the spirit world, and transmigration are still present even when not blended with traditional scholasticism. Although the transformation of these materials into the vocabulary of scientific humanism via the doctrine of anattā, atomic metaphysics, and the psychological benefits of the meditational yoga, etc., would seem to be an easy task, in fact, the socially grounded supernaturalism and magical animism of the tradition is deeply resistant to it. However, in all of this, it is clearly too soon to tell what new energies can be summoned from the spiritual isotopes latent in the teaching. The Western religions have been struggling with these problems for four hundred years, since the early Renaissance, and the outcome is still uncertain.

In China, after the imperial Confucian state finally forced Buddhism into its nonpolitical religious role, colonial intrusions had at first only a very indirect effect on the community. However, the T'ai-p'ing rebellion (1850-1864) in central China resulted in massive destruction and looting of many Buddhist centers; this shock proved to be a stimulus which moved both monks and laymen to develop a program of reconstruction in which Western values were introduced particularly through lay-managed Buddhist publishing houses and schools. The product of these innovations was a small Westernized Buddhist elite who developed reforming social interests, and some participated directly in the revolution against the oppressive Manchu regime in 1911.[22] Most striking was the work of the monk T'ai-hsü (1890-1947). He joined the revolutionary forces and founded voluntary lay groups for the promotion of democratic institutions, educational services, and Buddhist missions. He conceived of Buddhist universalism as the basis for social reform and ecumenical restoration of world peace and moral standards. He urged internal reforms in the Saṅgha, such as restoring monastic discipline and bringing the laity more actively into communal life.[23] However, T'ai-hsü was not supported in the main by the abbots of important Ch'an monasteries in central and south China, who on the whole regarded these secular involvements as violations of their traditional religious role. This stereotyped disinterest in political and social action can be ascribed in part to the fact that Buddhism had been formally excluded from a major part in Chinese national life for seven hundred years. The monastic orders had no stake in political ideology except where it intruded directly on their immediate welfare.

Under the Republic, Buddhism was afforded considerable religious freedom, and the statistics given for the community in 1930 show a huge cadre of over 700,000 monks and nuns distributed variously among 267,000 Buddhist temples and monastic centers. However, as the body of secularized and alienated Chinese intellectuals increased, there was mounting criticism of Buddhism along with Confucian traditionalism.[24] China and the Asian peoples as a whole had been victimized, so it was said, by the Western colonial powers because of the passive world-view inculcated by Buddhism. After the Japanese invasions in 1937, there were overt instances of Buddhist collaboration with the enemy because of the common religious tradition. All this engendered deeper hatred and mistrust.

In 1949 the Communist victory was followed by the confiscation of monastic properties and the forced return of thousands of monks and nuns to lay status and productive labor. However, the regime did not extirpate Buddhism, but instead placed it under rigorous ideological controls in the service of the state. The remaining monastic orders ostensibly retained their traditional customs; but the monks were employees of the state and served principally to support a public image of pacifist tolerance while the state pursued a rigorous campaign against Buddho-Taoist superstitions in the villages. The great architectural remains and other works of art were nationalized and maintained at government expense, representing the "spirit of the Chinese people" in the face of the feudal autocracies of the past. In 1953 the Buddhist Association of China with headquarters in Peking was formed, and it has systematically encouraged useful contacts with Buddhists in other lands, including the promotion of Buddhist scholarship and attendance at international meetings.[25] However, the revolution of Mao's Red Guards apparently resulted in new assaults on the Buddhist community including the extensive destruction of property and abusive treatment of monastic inmates, many of whom fled to Hong Kong and Formosa.

In Vietnam, Chinese Mahāyāna in the form of Ch'an and Pure Land penetrated deeply into the social fabric of Vietnamese life, and the monks were often bearers of Confucian culture as well. At the village level family ancestor worship and adherence to the five precepts were powerfully cohesive forces augmented by cultic practices in synthesis with local traditions.[26] The arrival of Catholic missionaries in the late sixteenth century was at first only loosely tied to Portuguese and French colonial policy. By the early eighteenth century there was a substantial Catholic minority—approximately 800,000. But the increasingly direct association of missionary activity with colonial exploitation provoked a nationalist response comparable in many respects to that of the other Buddhist states. This culminated in the Royalist Resistance Movement (1885-1898) centered around Buddhist values and promoted in many cases by revolutionary Buddhist monks.[27] The movement was suppressed but went underground in the form of numerous secret societies which, in turn, exacerbated the coercive practices of the French government and widened the gap between Catholics and Buddhists.

In the 1930s the Buddhist community began to develop new reforming interests promoted chiefly by a Westernized elite who were inspired by T'ai-hsü's example. The Cochinchina Buddhist Study Association was the source of a number of reforming movements which sponsored schools, hospitals, youth groups, newspapers, and social action programs—all deeply influenced by Western models.[28] At the same time, however, there were new syncretic religious movements—most notably the Cao Dai and Hoa Hao—which established provincial religious and political controls over sectors of the native population.[29] At the other extreme, the secularization of nationalist values and political ideologies was intensified by the indigenous Communist movement. The final defeat and withdrawal of the French in 1954 left Vietnam in a situation of precarious instability.

The revolutionary activities of the NLF on the one side and the rise of Ngo Dinh Diem on the other, placed the Buddhists in an extremely difficult ideological and political position. Diem, an ardent Catholic, came from an old Confucian mandarin family; his brother was an archbishop; and his techniques of political control were often autocratic and discriminatory. The involvement of the United States in the civil war added to the problem: first, because it appeared to many Buddhists to be another form of the old Catholic-colonial political system inimical to their own aspirations; and second because the Buddhists were particularly sensitized to the horrors of the conflict in the villages among the people whom they traditionally served.

In 1951—in the search for cultural and religious unity —the Buddhists had held a nationwide conference in Hué in an effort to unify the various Buddhist associations in the north and the south; but expectations were hopelessly shattered by the political realities.[30] In 1963 the Buddhist "revolts" against the Diem regime and the self-immolation of Buddhist monks represented the culmination of widely shared feelings of frustration and powerlessness which finally toppled the government.[31] The practice of self-immolation as a sacrificial expression of ultimate religious commitment and protest is not unknown to Mahāyāna tradition. In this case it served as an unmistakable if horrible symbol of the pathology of the larger situation, and was "rationally" designed to call attention to the martyrdom of Vietnam.

The long-range constructive potential of Buddhism in this situation is difficult to assess. In 1964 the Van Hanh University was instituted in Saigon with a joint Buddhist and secular faculty in which the School of Youth for Social Service is one of the most important divisions. But the role of the monastic orders in this kind of enterprise is less clear. A contemporary Vietnamese Buddhist monk observes that with few exceptions the monks "have been trained to recite sutras, to meditate, and to preach, and now become embarrassed at the role of responsible leadership suddenly thrust upon them."[32] As with Burma and Ceylon, the transition from an ideology of protest to one of modernizing construction is difficult, and in the current Vietnamese political situation effective stabilization of new values and goals is nearly impossible.

Tibet was not exposed to substantive Western acculturation, and remained steeped in the feudal theocratic tradition; but it continued to be troubled by political pressures emanating chiefly from China. It was bound closely to the Manchu dynasty, with the Chinese emperor appropriately designated an emanation of Mañjuśrī by the Dalai Lama, who served as his chaplain. During the Republic the high lamas continued to receive formal recognition from Chinese authorities, but traditional Chinese claims for political control in Tibet were overtly expressed in efforts to manipulate the Tibetan power structure—especially the cleavage between the Dalai and Panchen Lamas by favoring the latter and related political cliques. Latent hostilities were openly revealed during the early years of World War II when many Tibetans expressed the hope that the Japanese would win, since they were "within ones" (*nang ba*)—that is, presumed to be ardent Buddhists. After the Communist victory in China, the Peking government occupied Tibet in 1951, one year after the fourteenth Dalai Lama had been enthroned. They exploited the Tibetan theocracy by promoting the Panchen Lama to the vice-chairmanship of the Tibetan State Committee. After the Tibetan revolt and suppression in 1959, he was moved into the position of authority vacated by the Dalai Lama. Efforts to eliminate the economically unproductive aspects of feudal monasticism were abruptly instituted through the traditional theocratic lines of communication along with suitable propaganda and enforced controls from Peking. The Dalai Lama now resides in India as head of a large refugee Tibetan community. The fate of Buddhism in Tibet is comparable to that of its Chinese counterpart.[33]

In Japan, following Oda Nobunaga's short-lived dictatorship, the Tokugawa shoguns forced Buddhism into a utilitarian alignment with state policy. Through mandatory temple registration for all citizens, it was used to reinforce social controls against the encroachments of Christianity. After the Meiji restoration in 1868, it was further subordinated to the imperial Shintō-Confucian ideology. Shintō deities were divested of their "dual" association with bodhisattvas, and Buddhism in general was regarded as a foreign depredation on the purity of the indigenous religion.[34]

There is some indication that Pure Land devotionalism, together with Confucian and Shintō values, may have contributed to the psychological ethos which facilitated later rapid industrialization. A functional analogue has been established between the work ethic of ascetic Calvinism and certain forms of self-sacrificing Amida devotionalism found among businessmen of the Tokugawa and Meiji periods.[35] In the later Meiji and the early decades of the twentieth century the state promoted Buddhism extensively in Korea for the purpose of pacifying the conquered territory, while at the same time it intensified state Shintō teaching at home in support of nationalist aims.

The extraordinarily rapid modernization of Japan brought the techniques of Western European critical scholarship and philosophy into play during the late nineteenth century. The scholarly and often highly secularized exploration of Buddhist tradition was enhanced not only by the emergence of a strong professional intellectual elite, but by the fact that Buddhism was largely peripheral to state Shintō. Despite its forced alignment with national needs and its part in the Bushidō ethic, it was not directly identified by the state with a resurgent nationalist ideology, as was the case in Ceylon and Indochina. In addition, Japan was from the beginning the cultural recipient of many strands of Mahāyāna and Hīnayāna traditions, and was not bound by the philosophical orthodoxy of Theravāda. This variegated richness, in combination with Western acculturation, has been the source of new lines of creativity driven by a genuine search for meaning and value solidarity in the postwar situation—an extremely complex matrix of cultural ferment in which Buddhism appears in many old and new forms.[36]

Some of the traditional schools like Pure Land are still strongly institutionalized—with Jōdo claiming about 4 million adherents and Shin about 10 million. Some of the smaller schools like Shingon also retain solid social grounding. But the most striking feature of Buddhism in postwar Japan is the profusion of new sects and voluntary associations. They range from lay adaptations of Zen tradition—including meditation clubs formed by businessmen and students alike—to devotional cults which stress the magical health-giving properties of Buddhism for worldly success. Sōka Gakkai ("Value Creation Society") is a striking example of the synthesis of distinctive cultural traits, religious devotionalism, and innovative values.[37] Its growth has been phenomenal, penetrating through all social strata. It claims some 16 million adherents, including 150,000 non-Japanese and various missionary centers outside Japan. Political activism has transformed it into the third largest political party in Japan. Its aggressive solidarity is startling, and to many quite frightening, but it is an epitome of the striving for communally defined meaning in the vacuum of the postwar situation. It is based on a fusion of Nichiren's dogmatic teachings and a utilitarian philosophy which affirms worldly happiness, success, and well-being as valid spiritual goals. It is predominantly a lay organization, with a president who supervises a superbly organized "believers" bureaucracy with seemingly inexhaustible and genuinely ascetic energies. Priests of one of the Nichiren denominations act as leaders in worship and doctrine.

For Sōka Gakkai the purpose of human life is to find

worldly happiness in personal health, security, wealth, family, and friends. This rationale was defined in the writings of the founder, Makiguchi Tsunesaburō (1871-1944). Apparent affirmations of dominant worldly values are deeply immersed in religious symbols which validate long-range striving for personal and social reconstruction. The principal medium for attaining this end is neither a rational idealism nor hedonism but, rather, absolute faith in the "Worship Object"—specifically, in the *Lotus Sūtra* as defined by Nichiren and his writings. Around this core there is an array of ancillary techniques of worship and education. False belief is as bad as no belief—and all other religions are derogated as harshly as Nichiren did. The expressed goal of the movement is the conversion of Japan and the world, and the final elimination of all human misery. The value of suffering is that it leads to belief; it is not a final or even appropriate aspect of the human condition in itself. The mythopoeic roots of the teaching are grounded jointly in the classical theory of historical degeneration and karma: transmigration is real, but in this degenerate age it can be controlled through faith and inspired worship. Karmic merit is acquired on this basis most saliently through missionary activity. Spiritual status and prestige in the community are directly the result of converting others to the true religion. It includes not only generalized preaching, but "forced-conversion" intimidation and direct threats of personal misfortune, sickness, financial reversals, and even earthquakes. The magical properties of faith ensure continued health or recovery from sickness, the forestalling of death, and many other benefits. The inevitable exceptions are, of course, ascribed to a lack of faith. For a true believer, final death holds no fears, since he has attained the immortal "Buddha-mind" and its perfections. The otherworldly "heavens" of Pure Land are regarded as detestable admissions of failure in this world.

All of these values are promoted and acted out in an extraordinarily vital communal setting which would doubtless have fascinated Émil Durkheim. "Value creation," group solidarity, and personal security are clearly the result of shared symbols continuously reinforced through ritual and worship, testimonials, pep-songs, pageants, sports, and specific affirmations of communal power through direct political action aimed at transforming Japan into a theocratic state. High value is placed on national interests within the religious framework of Nichiren's world-view. Lines of authority are strict, but structured within the community like the Marxist cell-system so that all members feel direct participation in the movement. The militant ethos has provoked bitter criticism and charges of religious bigotry and political fascism. However, the founders of the movement were imprisoned by the Tōjō regime for criticizing the worship of the emperor, and political goals have not been aligned with a narrow or conservative nationalism. The political arm of the community describes itself simply as the "Clean Government Party."[38]

In all of this it is impossible to miss the immense residual importance of the Japanese group-nexus and the search for personal security, success, power, and directed meaning through hierarchical affiliations which combine authority, sociability, and religious certainties. The family is not the principal building block. The believer is expected to try to convert family members too, but the movement cuts across traditional ascriptive institutions and builds solidarities of the lonely, anxious, and alienated—for instance, in its very strong youth movement and among women whose evangelistic role is far removed from the traditional image of silence and obedience. Other factors include the obvious business advantages to be shared by members who are assured that the maximization of economic power is a positive religious good, perhaps in the face of lurking uncertainties about the meaning of it all.

The religious and political militance of Sōka Gakkai is rejected by other sects which, nevertheless, share some of the same general values. The Risshō Kōseikai ("Cooperative Self-fulfillment Society") for example, is a lay movement which also centers its activities around the *Lotus Sūtra* as a means for solving problems of personal adjustment amid the alienating pressures of the industrial city, but it eschews the Nichiren form of religious absolutism.[39]

At the other end of this wide cultural spectrum we find philosophical syntheses of Western and Buddhist categories in the work of men like Nishida Kitarō and Kawakami Hajime.[40] Perhaps the most remarkable example of refined philosophical and historical reflection is to be found in the works of Ienaga Saburō (1906-   ).[41] Ienaga sees in the history of Japanese Buddhism—particularly in Shōtoku and Shinran—evidence of its transcendent universalism and capacity to cut through traditional forms with innovating power; but this is paradoxically mixed with an easy accommodation to the givenness of the world and a loss of critical tension, with worldly institutions either simply affirmed or regarded as inherently illusory and unreal. Ienaga's powerful critique of Buddhist tradition is extended to Japanese culture in general and to human religious history itself. He points to the endemic human tendency to construe evil and imperfection as the result of incorrect beliefs, external forces, or improper ethics. On the contrary, evil and suffering are not epiphenomena, but are of the essence of life and will emerge despite all magical, yogic, or dogmatic panaceas through the crushing grind of human history. Man's recognition of his finitude and weakness will be forced upon him as an absolutely inescapable religious insight. So, for example, Ienaga mistrusts what he construes to be the normative Zen search for a transcending "pure experience" in the unity of the self and the world—a euphoric "beyond good and evil" which then ironically validates the given conditions and institutions of the times. The paradoxical contradictions and brutalities of life must be faced directly, before faith, moral striving, or mysticism make sense—and even then these forms may become idolized and self-destructive rituals.

In the West the influence of Buddhism and more generally of Indian culture has been many-sided. The ancient Middle East, particularly in various forms of Islamic mysticism and philosophy, clearly reflects the incorporation of Indian as well as Hellenistic values. In the colonial and postcolonial eras in Western Europe the influx of Asian religious traditions made a profound impact. The purely academic scrutiny of Buddhist and Hindu literature via linguistic and historical study was combined with a deeper mood of receptivity created by the postenlightenment corrosion of traditional religious values and ecclesiastical authority. This was accompanied by a growing interest in those aspects of Indian tradition which stressed the religious and philosophical autonomy of the self—especially the yoga, and speculative and experimental mysticism. And there were many lines of convergence with the interests of the romantic philosophers, Western mysticism, and oriental studies.[42] The central element, however, was the search for individual freedom and personal meaning in a culture regarded as ravaged by conflict, dehumanizing materialism, and the loss of traditional religious moorings.

The influence of Buddhism and Indian mysticism in the West can be seen first in such diverse nineteenth-century movements as the Theosophical Society, the New England Transcendentalists, and later in the specific institutionalization of various Hindu and Buddhist Associations in England, Europe, and America. In Germany it is possible to trace the effects of Buddhist acculturation in many areas, for instance, in literature and philosophy from Schopenhauer to Herman Hesse.[43]

Zen Buddhism, in particular, as expounded by D. T. Suzuki and Western enthusiasts, has had a positive resonance with existentialism and psychoanalysis,[44] though, popular adaptations of Zen teaching have often been marked by a facile dilletantism, and occasionally seem steeped in a miasma of oriental coloration and pseudomorphs exploited and commercialized by the very forces which it seeks to renounce. The market for orientalia is now a multimillion-dollar business, often most apparent in college campus bookstores. It nevertheless has just as often seemed in basic accord with the classical features of naturalistic mysticism and practical simplicity which affirms the therapeutic power of latent spiritual forces yet to be awakened in the self. For many young people the prolonged state of adolescence, induced in part by formal expectations of "higher education" amid excruciating uncertainties about the meaning of it all, has evoked a deep interest in many forms of Indian and East Asian spirituality. The painful search for personal identity has often been positively mediated merely by the atmosphere of religious techniques which impute direct spiritual value to the inner anxieties and dynamics of maturation in the face of institutional artificialities and restraints.

Within this value framework one can detect a tendency to passive withdrawal and sociopolitical quietism which is nevertheless frequently mixed with a deep and pervasive moral concern making itself known without overt aggression. It appears as a relatively gentle critique of given cultural values and adult roles, and is largely uncongenial to Marxist inspired activism and other ideologies of violence.

The institutionalization of this diffuse culture in America has taken many forms which provide a rich but as yet nearly untapped reservoir for field study and research. It ranges from well-financed cults, *āshrams*, and yoga centers, to informal associations, shading off into fashionable mannerisms, symbols, and attire, which nevertheless are evidence of a pervasive uneasiness and the search for new and more authentic modes of self-expression.[45]

It is impossible to predict in what direction these ill-defined and free-floating forms will move. With the exception of a few professional and often well-paid adepts, its leadership is unorganized and largely unknown; and it is cross-cut with experimental interests in drugs and "dropout" communalism. What we can most probably expect in the long run is a synthesis of psychoanalytic and Buddhist insights which will be increasingly relevant to an affluent but anxiety-ridden society in which the meaning of life and the self loom as overwhelming concerns no longer manageable through traditional religious media. The prospect of technological advances which reduce the needs for human labor and increase leisure time for self-reflection would seem to place additional value on the autonomous and exploratory focus of the yoga in all its immensely varied forms. However, proof of its adequacy as a systematic life-method for the reconstruction of human values and the transformation of the self and society has by no means been clear in the historical past. Furthermore, selfish withdrawal, complacency, hypocrisy, and pride hidden under the cloak of yogic piety and mystical striving cannot be easily eradicated by popularly consumable assertions about its presumed relevance to long-range personal and social health.

Nevertheless, the basic model of man, and the richly developed psycho-metaphysical symbolism present within this ancient tradition, is an immensely promising sphere for the creative explorations imperatively needed both now and in the future.

Notes

INTRODUCTION

1. Max Weber, *The Religion of India* (Glencoe, Ill., 1958), pp. 206, 233. Weber, *Sociology of Religion* (Glencoe, Ill., 1960) introduction by Talcott Parsons.
2. Cf., for example, the rather different positions taken on the Weber thesis by D. E. Smith and E. Sarkisyanz in their respective interpretations of the role of Buddhism in Burma: *Religion and Politics in Burma* (Princeton, 1965), pp. 7, 323-324, and *The Buddhist Background of the Burmese Revolution* (The Hague, 1965), pp. 37, 39, 43, 56. See H. Bechert, "Einige Fragen der Religions Soziologie und Struktur des Suedasiastischen Buddhismus," *International Yearbook for the Sociology of Religion*, 4 (1968), pp. 251-253; a detailed discussion of Weber's perspective.
3. Max Weber, *The Protestant Ethic and the Spirit of Capitalism* (New York, 1958), p. 182.

1. INDIA

1. See K. Jaspers, *The Origin and Goal of History* (New Haven, 1953), especially his reconstruction of the "axial period" (800-200 B.C.), and R. N. Bellah, "Religious Evolution," in *Beyond Belief* (New York, 1970), pp. 20-50.
2. C. Drekmeier, *Kingship and Community in Early India* (Stanford, 1962), pp. 12-88.
3. *Muṇḍaka Upaniṣad*, I. ii. 7-13, adapted from R. E. Hume (trans.), *The Thirteen Principal Upanishads* (London, 1921).
4. E. Lamotte, *Histoire du Bouddhisme Indien* (Louvain, 1958), pp. 13-25, a concise review of the critical issues.
5. See W. Geiger, *Pāli Dhamma* (Munich, 1920); T. Stcherbatsky, *The Central Conception of Buddhism and the Meaning of the Word "Dharma"* (London, 1923).
6. *Digha Nikāya*, I, 83, ed. T. W. Rhys Davids and J. E. Carpenter, 3 vols., Pāli Text Society (PTS) (London, 1890-1911). See the fuller version in the *Saṃyutta Nikāya*, V,

421ff. ed. L. Feer and T. W. Rhys Davids, PTS, 6 vols. (London, 1884-1904). In citing Theravāda sources we use the Pāli form, elsewhere the Sanskrit.

7. *Dhammapada*, vss. 188-192, ed. C. Rhys Davids, in *Minor Anthologies of the Pāli Canon* (London, 1931).

8. *Majjhima Nikāya*, I, 256ff., ed. V. Trenckner and R. Chalmers, PTS, 3 vols. (London, 1888-1899).

9. *Ibid.*, I, 420ff.; cf. the *Mettā Sutta* from the *Sutta Nipata*, ed. D. Anderson and H. Smith, PTS (London, 1913).

10. *Digha Nikāya*, II, 64ff. See T. Stcherbatsky, *The Conception of Buddhist Nirvāṇa* (Leningrad, 1927).

11. *Dhammapada*, v. 287.

12. See A. Bareau, *Les premiers conciles bouddhiques* (Paris, 1955).

13. See H. Oldenberg and T. W. Rhys Davids, *Vinaya Texts*, in F. M. Müller (ed.), *Sacred Books of the East* (Oxford, 1881-1885), vols. 13, 17, 20.

14. *Dhammapada*, v. 194.

15. Lamotte, *Histoire*, pp. 312ff.

16. Cf. *The Mahaparinibbāna Sutta*, in *Digha Nikāya* II, 99ff.

17. *Digha Nikāya*, II, 49; actually designated a "patimokkha" (prātimokṣa), also *Dhammapada*, vss. 184-185.

18. *Dhammapada*, vv. 73-75. See S. Dutt, *Early Buddhist Monachism* (London, 1924).

19. Lamotte, *Histoire*, pp. 713ff.; J. Masson, *La Religion populaire dans le canon bouddhique Pāli* (Louvain, 1942).

20. *Digha Nikāya*, III, 18off.

21. *Sutta Nipata*, v. 136; systematic refutations of Brāhmanic caste doctrine appear in the *Digha Nikāya*, III, 8off., and in the *Majjhima Nikāya*, II, 147ff.

22. *Digha Nikāya*, III, 58ff. It attributes political and social degeneration to the moral failures of monarchs who use coercion in lieu of exemplary personal leadership. Cf. B. G. Gokhale, "Early Buddhist View of the State," *Journal of the American Oriental Society*, LXXXIX, No. 4 (1969).

23. J. Bloch, *Les Inscriptions d'Asoka* (Paris, 1950), Rock Edict XIII, Pillar Edict VII, Separate Kalinga Edict I.

24. *Dhammapada*, vv. 103, 24. Hindu tradition also has comparable *Rajadharma* ("King's Law") teachings. See Drekmeier, *op. cit.*, chs. 8, 9.

25. Bloch, *op. cit.*, Rock Edict XI. See R. Thapar, *Asoka and the Decline of the Mauryas* (Oxford University Press, 1961).

26. The Aśoka tradition was perpetuated in Buddhist literature, serving as a paradigm of royal piety and political values.

See P. H. L. Eggermont, *The Chronology of the Reign of Asoka Moriya* (Leiden, 1956), for a concise summary of these materials in their Theravādin, Mahāyāna and Tibetan sources; and J. Przyluski, *La Légende de l'empereur Açoka* (Paris, 1923).

27. See Lamotte, *Histoire*, pp. 385ff., 489ff., 726ff.

28. Lamotte, "Sur la formation du Mahāyāna," *Asiatica*, Festscrift Weller (Leipzig, 1954), pp. 381-386.

29. H. Dayal, *The Bodhisattva Doctrine in Buddhist Sanskrit Literature* (London, 1932).

30. Śāntideva (*ca.* A.D. 650), *Śikṣāsmuccaya*; adapted from E. Conzé (ed.), *Buddhist Texts through the Ages* (New York, 1964), pp. 131-132. The "vow" to forgo immediate personal salvation for the sake of helping other creatures was, in many cases, a sufficient substitute for monastic ordination. In this way institutional formalities and monastic immobility were partially bypassed, and the layman could be a dynamic and spiritually sanctified agent of salvation.

31. See T. V. Murti, *The Central Philosophy of Buddhism* (London, 1955).

32. Asaṅga (*ca.* A.D. 350), *Mahāyānasaṃgraha*, II, 27; adapted from Lamotte, *La somme du grand vehicule d'Asaṅga* (Louvain, 1939).

33. "Tathāgata" is a traditional epithet of the Buddha. It is of uncertain etymology—perhaps literally "thus gone," signifying total spiritual perfection and emancipation. In this new form its original meaning is drastically altered, since the Buddha is now the living, fecund ground of being.

34. See A. Foucher, *L'Art Greco-bouddhique du Gandhara*, 2 vols. (Paris, 1905-1923).

35. Sāramati, *Ratnagotravibhāga*, I, v. 28; in Conzé, *Buddhist Texts*, p. 181.

36. Asaṅga, *Mahāyānasūtrālaṅkāra*, IX, 60-66, T. W. deBary (ed.), *Sources of the Indian Tradition* (New York, 1960), pp. 175-176. The term "Dharmakāya" originally signified the specific doctrine expounded by the Buddha—the worldly remnant of his sojourn on earth. But in this new framework it is an ontological essence inseparable from the active presence of the Buddha's saving power.

37. *Saddharmapuṇḍarīka*, III, 27, adapted from H. Kern in F. M. Müller (ed.), *Sacred Books of the East*, vol. 21 (Oxford, 1884).

38. *Vimalakīrtinirdeśa*, II, adapted from Lamotte, *L'Enseignement de Vimalakīrti* (Louvain, 1962).

39. *Suvarṇaprabhāsottama Sūtra*, VI, deBary, *Sources of the Indian Tradition*, pp. 184-187.

40. S. B. Dasgupta, *An Introduction to Tantric Buddhism* (Calcutta, 1950), pp. 214-215; "People die through the passions, and are again liberated through the passions, . . . this is unknown . . . to the ordinary orthodox Buddhists" (*Hevajra Tantra*).

41. Saraha, *Dohākoṣa*, vss. 47-48, in Conzé, *Buddhist Texts*, p. 230; see M. Eliade, *Yoga* (Princeton, 1970), pp. 227ff. on *Haṭhayoga*.

42. *Cittaviśuddhiprakaraṇa*, in deBary, *Sources of the Indian Tradition*, p. 198.

43. See especially the *Guhyasamaja Tantra*, in Conzé, *op. cit.*, pp. 221-224; cf. Dasgupta, *op. cit.*, pp. 80, 202; and M. Eliade, *Yoga* (Princeton, 1970), p. 205.

44. Saraha, *Dohākoṣa*, v. 46: "naü sudda ṇa vamhaṇa," which Snellgrove translates "neither outcaste nor Brāhman" in Conzé, *Buddhist Texts*, p. 230. The *Hevajra Tantra* specifically refers to the consort as a *ḍombi*—an outcaste washerwoman. See Dasgupta, *op. cit.*, pp. 114, 141.

45. A traditional distinction is often made between "Left-Hand" (erotic) and "Right-Hand" Tantric practices. Tantric cults in the latter category eschew the sexual rites. The distinction applies to Hindu tradition as well.

46. Eliade, *Yoga*, (New York, 1959), p. 214.

47. Dasgupta, *op. cit.*, pp. 72ff.

48. Saraha: "The Brāhmans who do not know truth, vainly recite the four Vedas," in Conzé, *Buddhist Texts*, p. 224.

49. See R. C. Mitra, *The Decline of Buddhism in India* (Calcutta, 1954).

2.   CHINA

1. E. Zürcher, *The Buddhist Conquest of China*, 2 vols (Leiden, 1959), vol. I, chs. 1-2.

2. See K. Chen, *Buddhism in China* (Princeton, 1964), pp. 21-27; and A. Wright, *Buddhism in Chinese History* (Stanford, 1959), pp. 11ff.

3. Cf. D. Holzman, *La Vie et la pensée de Hi K'ang* (Leiden, 1957); and E. Balazs, "Entre révolte nihiliste et évasion mystique," *Études Asiatiques*, 2 (1948), 34-40.

4. "The Memorial of Hsiang K'ai," in Zürcher, *op. cit.*, vol. I, pp. 37-38.

5. A. Wright, "Fo-t'u-teng: A Biography," *Harvard Journal of Asiatic Studies*, XI (1948), 352.

6. J. Takakusu and K. Watanabe (eds.), *Taishō Shinshu Dai-zōkyō*, vol. 52, 1-7 (*Li-huo-lun in Hung-ming chi*), 85 vols. (Tokyo, 1914-1932); hereafter designated *Taishō*. See Zürcher, *op. cit.*, ch. 6 on the Buddho-Taoist conflict. Mou-tzu's dates are uncertain, but the conflict remained endemic.

7. Zürcher, *op. cit.*, p. 228; see P. Demiéville, "La Pénétration du bouddhisme dans la tradition philosophique chinoise," *Cahiers d'histoire mondiale*, 3, I (1956), 19-38.

8. See Chih-tun's "*Eulogy on the Image of the Buddha*," Zürcher, *op. cit.*, pp. 177-179.

9. Chen, *op. cit.*, pp. 113, 367-368, 382-385.

10. On the Tun-huang caves see P. Pelliot, *Les Grottes de Touen-houang*, 6 vols. (Paris, 1914-1924); S. Muzuno and T. Nagahiro, *Yun-kang*, 16 vols. (Kyoto, 1951-1956), with superb plates.

11. Zürcher, *op. cit.*, p. 153.

12. *Taishō*, vol. 52, 29-32 (*Sha-men pu-ching wang-che lun*, in *Hung-ming chi*). See Zürcher's complete translation of Hui-yüan's biography, *op. cit.*, pp. 240-253.

13. Letter #15 of 18 letters (*ca.* A.D. 405-409) together with Kumarājīva's answers summarized by Zürcher, *op. cit.*, pp. 226-229.

14. Wright, "The Formation of Sui Ideology," in J. Fairbank (ed.), *Chinese Thought and Institutions* (Chicago, 1957), pp. 93-104.

15. See Chen, *op. cit.*, pp. 241ff.

16. See L. Hurvitz, *Chih-i*, Mélanges chinois et bouddhiques, XII (Bruges, 1963).

17. *Taishō*, vol. 45, 663-667 (*Chin-shih-tzu chang*); J. Takakusu, *The Essentials of Buddhist Philosophy* (Honolulu, 1947), pp. 108-125.

18. See Chen, *op. cit.*, pp. 338-349; and Takakusu, *op. cit.*, pp. 170ff.

19. *Taishō*, vol. 47, 8-11 (*An-lo chi*); see T. W. deBary (ed.), *Sources of the Chinese Tradition* (New York, 1960), ch. 17.

20. On the issues surrounding Bodhidharma and early Ch'an, see H. Dumoulin, "Bodhidharma und die Anfange des Ch'an Buddhismus," *Monumenta Nipponica*, 7 (1951), 63-83; Hu Shih, "*Development of Zen Buddhism in China*," *Chinese Social and Political Science Review*, 15 (1931), 475-505.

21. P. Yampolsky, *The Platform Sūtra of the Sixth Patriarch* (New York, 1947). Note variant on second line ("Since originally there is nothing, whereon could dust fall?").

22. *Ching-te ch'uan teng lu*, 30, 6b-7 (*Hsien-tsung chi*), Ssu-pu ts'ung-k'an, series 3 (SPTK) (Shanghai, 1935). And "calmness is no calmness, wisdom no wisdom . . . ."

23. *Ibid.*, 30, 8a. Shen-hui also waged a vigorous campaign against the northern ("gradualist") school and helped to support the imperial house in war efforts during the An Lu-shan rebellion (A.D. 755) by public fund-raising.

24. Pen-chi (840-901); *Taishō*, vol. 47, 537-539 (*Ts'ao-shan Pen-chi ch'an-shih yü-lu*), Kung-an #4.

25. On Chinese Tantrism see Chen, *op. cit.*, pp. 332-337. It is difficult to assess to what extent the deeply embedded moral conservatism of Confucianism actually inhibited the development of radical Tantrism or simply suppressed the data. The Chen-yen ("True Word," Mantrayāna) school was clearly in the "Right-Hand" esoteric tradition.

26. See J. Gernet, *Les Aspects économique du Bouddhisme dans la société Chinoise du Ve au Xe siècle* (Saigon, 1956), pp. 297-298.

27. See Wright, *Buddhism*, ch. 5. He concludes: "Despite its occasional use for political purposes—e.g., to sanctify power and justify war—it was prevented by its basic postulate of the delusive and transitory character of earthly existence from developing a comprehensive political theory." This is basically Max Weber's thesis; but it must be carefully guarded. When the Chinese patrimonial state and Confucian elite decided to exclude Buddhism from a central role in the polity, there was no lay social bloc capable of stopping it. Whereas in Southeast Asia and Tibet (see below, ch. 3) the politicization of Buddhism took place in favorable cultural milieux, "illusionist" postulate and all.

28. The Sung rulers contributed to the decline of the Saṅgha by selling monastic offices and certificates which exempted the bearer from corvée and taxation. See Chen, *op. cit.*, pp. 391-402.

29. See Chen, *op. cit.*, pp. 426ff., and the interesting passage on the "laughing Buddha" (Mo-li-fo, Maitreya) as an epitome of "worldly" Chinese values, pp. 405ff. Cf. Wright, *Buddhism*, pp. 99ff.

3. SOUTHEAST ASIA AND TIBET

1. W. Rahula, *History of Buddhism in Ceylon* (Colombo, 1966), pp. 10ff., 48-50. H. Bechert, "Theravāda Buddhist

Saṅgha," *Journal of Asian Studies*, XXIX, 4 (August, 1970), pp. 761-778.

2. Rahula, *op. cit.*, chs. 9-10, on the growth of the feudal and administrative structure in the Saṅgha; a remarkable example of the rationalization of Indian tradition to suit Sinhalese socioeconomic and political needs.

3. *Mahāvaṃsa*, trans. W. Geiger (London, 1912), I, 58ff.; XIV, 38-41.

4. *Mahāvaṃsa*, XX, 14-15; Rahula, *op. cit.*, pp. 58ff.; on the Brāhmans, p. 43; caṇḍalas (outcastes) performed menial "sanitation" tasks, pp. 17ff., and ch. 14.

5. *Mahāvaṃsa*, XXI, 22-26.

6. *Ibid.*, XXV, 108-111.

7. Rahula, *op. cit.*, pp. 82-101, 107. One of the crimes attributed to the Mahāsuññavāda sounds Vajrayānist: sexual relations may be entered into by any consenting human pair.

8. N. Ray, *Theravāda Buddhism in Burma* (Calcutta, 1946), pp. 99-100; D. Smith, *Religion and Politics in Burma* (Princeton, 1965), p. 13; H. Bechert, *op. cit.*, pp. 764-765.

9. G. Coedès, *The Making of South East Asia* (Berkeley, 1967), pp. 50ff., 8off. On the prehistoric background, see Coedès, ch. 2; D. G. E. Hall, *History of South East Asia* (New York, 1968), pp. 8-9; E. Seifenfaden, *The Thai Peoples* (Bangkok, 1958), p. 58; K. Landon, *South East Asia* (Chicago, 1959), pp. 25ff.

10. L. Briggs, *The Ancient Khmer Empire* (Philadelphia, 1951), pp. 41, 52, 90, 105-106, 126, 167; Hall, *op. cit.*, pp. 97ff., 108-109.

11. Ray, *op. cit.*, pp. 147-151; this "Tantric" sect (the "Aris") was highly syncretic and also politically independent, with a warrior elite.

12. H. Q. Wales, *Ancient Siamese Government and Administration* (London, 1934), pp. 69, 177.

13. W. Vella, *Siam under Rama III* (Locust Valley, N.Y., 1957), pp. 9-10; see Wales, *op. cit.*, ch. 8.

14. Chou Ta-kuan, *Memoires on the Customs of Cambodia*, in Hall, *op. cit.*, p. 125.

15. Coedès, *Recueil des Inscriptions du Siam* (Bangkok, 1924), vol. I, p. 77, #11; and see Coedès, *The Making of South East Asia*, pp. 126ff., "The Crisis of the Thirteenth Century."

16. Coedès, *The Making of South East Asia*, pp. 46ff.; Thich Nhat Hanh, *Vietnam* (New York, 1967), ch. 2.

17. Hall, *op. cit.*, chs. 3-4.

18. *Ibid.*, pp. 42ff. The Chinese pilgrim I-tsing reports that "Hīnayāna" also was widespread in the archipelago (*ca.* 650); but it was an item of discrete study rather than a bureaucratized monastic system. J. Takakusu, *A Record of the Buddhist Religion* (London, 1896).

19. P. Mus, *"Barabudur," Bulletin de l'École Français* (BEFEO), 32 (1923), no. 1, pp. 269-439.

20. Coedès, *Pour Mieux Comprendre Angkor* (Paris, 1947), chs. 3, 8); the symbolism is intended to deify members of the royal family.

21. Hall, *op. cit.*, p. 217.

22. H. Hoffman, *The Religions of Tibet* (New York, 1961), chs. 1, 5. The problems of historical reconstruction are complicated by the fact that the Bön elite later appropriated Buddhist doctrine and practice; see D. Snellgrove (trans. and ed.), *The Nine Ways of Bon* (London, 1967), introduction.

23. R. Ekvall, *Religious Observances in Tibet* (Chicago, 1964), pp. 2-9.

24. On the archaic shamanistic background, see F. W. Thomas, *Tibetan Literary Texts and Documents concerning Chinese Turkestan*, 3 vols. (London, 1935-1955), vol. I, pp. 268-295; and his *Ancient Folk Literature from Northeastern Tibet* (Berlin, 1957), pp. 113-157; R. Nebesky-Wojkowitz, *Oracles and Demons of Tibet* (The Hague, 1956), pp. 417-443; R. A. Stein, *Le Civilisation Tibétain* (Paris, 1962), pp. 209ff.; and G. Tucci, *Tibetan Painted Scrolls*, 2 vols. (Rome, 1949), vol. I, pp. 713ff.

25. The chronicle of Bu-ston (1290-1364) traces the early history of Tibet through the development of the great theocracy; trans. E. Obermiller, *The History of Buddhism* (Heidelberg, 1931), vol. II, pp. 183-224; see Hoffman, *op. cit.*, pp. 36ff., for a concise and insightful survey.

26. The Padmasambhava tradition is complex and fragmentary. See G. C. Toussaint (trans.), *Le Dict de Padma* (Paris, 1933); Stein, *L'épopée tibétaine de Gesar* (Paris, 1956), also translated by A. David-Neel (Paris, 1931, 1933); W. Y. Evans-Wentz, *The Tibetan Book of the Great Liberation* (New York, 1969), p. 105-192.

27. Evans-Wentz, *op. cit.*, pp. 119-120, 141-142, 182-191.

28. P. Demiéville, *Le Concile de Lhasa* (Paris, 1952); see Hoffman, *op. cit.*, pp. 74ff.

29. A. Chattopadhyaya, *Atiśa and Tibet* (Calcutta, 1967).

30. J. Bacot, *Le poète tibétain Milarepa* (Paris, 1925), a translation of a biography ascribed to one of his pupils; and Hoffman, *Mi-la Ras-pa* (Munich, 1950).

31. Trans. D. Snellgrove, in Conzé, *Buddhist Texts*, pp. 258, 260.

32. See E. Obermiller, *Tsong-kha-pa le Pandit*, Mélanges chinois et bouddhique, vol. III (Brussels, 1935); and Hoffman, *Religions*, ch. 8. The fourteenth century also saw the codification of the canonical materials in two great collections: the *Kanjur* ("Translation of the Buddha's Word") and the *Tanjur* ("Translation of the Text Books"). This body of material contains an immense spectrum of Hīnayāna, Mahāyāna, and Tantric sources.

33. See Hoffman, *Religions*, pp. 168-170.

34. *Ibid.*, pp. 173ff.

35. On the theocracy and land control see P. Carrasco, *Land and Polity in Tibet* (Seattle, 1959), pp. 78-84, and the concept of the "authority center."

36. Ekvall, *op. cit.*, chs. 4-8; especially, on violence and anxiety vis-à-vis the therapy of circumambulation, pp. 247-248.

37. *Ibid.*, pp. 163-198; and Carrasco, *op. cit.*, on the economics of "giving."

4. JAPAN

1. See J. E. Kidder, *Japan before Buddhism* (London, 1959); and G. B. Sansom, *Japan* (London, 1952), ch. 1, pp. 36-44, 54.

2. *Nihongi*, vol. II, p. 66, trans. W. G. Aston, *Chronicles of Japan*, 2 vols. (London, 1896).

3. *Ibid.*, pp. 121-123; see M. Anesaki, *History of Japanese Religion* (Tokyo, 1963), pp. 57-60. M. W. de Visser, *Ancient Buddhism in Japan*, 2 vols. (Leiden, 1935).

4. *Ibid.*, pp. 128-131, articles 2, 3, 4, 7, 10. See H. Bohner *Shōtoku Taishi* (Tokyo, 1940). The critical problems surrounding the actual content of Shōtoku's contributions are still being debated. See J. H. Kamstra, *Encounter or Syncretism: The Initial Growth of Japanese Buddhism* (Leiden, 1967).

5. See Sansom, *op. cit.*, pp. 73ff., on the rigidity of the clan system.

6. On the Taika ("great innovation") reform, see Sansom, *op. cit.*, ch. 5, and Anesaki, *op. cit.*, pp. 79ff.

7. W. T. deBary (ed.), *Sources of the Japanese Tradition* (New York, 1960), pp. 100-101.

8. On the Nara sects, see the review in Anesaki, *op. cit.*, pp. 86-104.

9. As in the Chinese case (see above, p. 71), the Buddhist metaphysic was not only "useful" but positively therapeutic for the ruling elite.

10. Sansom, *op. cit.*, pp. 184ff.

11. deBary, *op. cit.*, p. 118. Mahāyāna (i.e., the Lotus) is described as "positive" in contrast with the "negative" teachings of Theravāda (the ideal of self-extinction—anattā). See C. Eliot, *Japanese Buddhism* (New York, 1959), ch. 14.

12. In deBary, *op. cit.*, p. 130; and see "Saicho's Vow of Uninterrupted Study of the Lotus Sutra," in deBary, pp. 128-129.

13. *Ibid.*, pp. 141-142. In the Ten Stages hierarchy the rudimentary condition of man (in the "first stage") is described in summary: "How could the great Enlightened One, feeling a fatherly compassion for all sentient beings and seeing the misery of their existence, silently let it pass?"

14. On Shingon legitimation of "warrior" symbols, see Anesaki, *op. cit.*, pp. 146-147, and on the deepening social crisis, pp. 160-169; Sansom, *op. cit.*, pp. 263-269.

15. See Anesaki, *op. cit.*, pp. 156-157; deBary, *op. cit.*, pp. 283ff. The mood of aesthetic pessimism is revealed in the opening lines of *The Tale of the Heike*: "The temple bell echoes the impermanence of all things. The colors of the flowers testify to the truth that those who flourish must decay" (Sansom, *op. cit.*, p. 295).

16. Sansom, on the rise of the Samurai, *op. cit.*, pp. 270ff.

17. Eliot, *op. cit.*, chs. 10, 16; Sansom, *op. cit.*, pp. 244ff.; Anesaki, *op. cit.*, pp. 170ff.

18. deBary, *op. cit.*, pp. 198-199.

19. *Ibid.*, pp. 196-197.

20. Trans. in H. Coates and R. Ishizuaka, *Hōnen the Buddhist Saint* (Tokyo, 1930), pp. 728-729.

21. Trans. in A. Lloyd, *Shinran and His Works* (Tokyo, 1910), pp. 47-49.

22. Anesaki, *Nichiren, the Buddhist Prophet* (Cambridge, Mass., 1916).

23. *Ibid.*, cited on p. 115. He identifies himself with the bodhisattva Viśiṣṭacārita.

24. Trans. in A. Lloyd, *The Creed of Half Japan* (London, 1911), pp. 316-318.

25. Anesaki, *Nichiren*, cited p. 74. See Eliot, *op. cit.*, ch. 18.

26. Eliot, *op. cit.*, ch. 17; deBary, *op. cit.*, pp. 241-243; Sansom, *op. cit.*, pp. 339ff.; Anesaki, *History*, pp. 206ff.

27. deBary, *op. cit.*, pp. 251-253, 255-256.

28. *Ibid.*, p. 247.
29. See Eliot, *op. cit.*, pp. 294-296, and Anesaki, *History*, pp. 223-224.
30. Sansom, *op. cit.*, p. 377; Anesaki, *History*, pp. 231ff.
31. Sansom, *op. cit.*, pp. 406ff.; Eliot, *op. cit.*, p. 300; Anesaki, *History*, p. 233. Nobunaga contemplated "divine-kingship" status, but was assassinated before he could put his plans into action.

5. ASPECTS OF THE CONTEMPORARY SITUATION

1. See K. Morgan (ed.), *The Path of Buddha* (New York, 1956), selected essays by contemporary Buddhists which reflect (often indirectly) these and other issues; also J. Schechter, *The New Face of the Buddha* (New York, 1967); and C. Moore, "Buddhism and Science," in S. Yamaguchi (ed.), *Buddhism and Culture* (Kyoto, 1960), pp. 89-125.
2. See Ray, *op. cit.*, pp. 248-249; and D. E. Smith, *Religion and Politics in Burma* (Princeton, 1965), pp. 157-164.
3. E. Zelliot, "Buddhism and Politics in Maharashtra," in D. E. Smith (ed.), *South Asian Politics and Religion* (Princeton, 1969), pp. 191-212; D. Keer, *Dr. Ambedkar, Life and Mission* (Bombay, 1962).
4. Cited by Zelliot, *op. cit.*, p. 195. Ambedkar also published a newspaper to represent his views, *Mooknayak* ("Voice of the Dumb").
5. See his excoriation of Gandhi in *What Congress and Gandhi Have Done to the Untouchables* (Bombay, 1946), chs. 10-11.
6. See D. E. Smith, *India as a Secular State* (Princeton, 1963), pp. 322-326.
7. The oath which he and his followers took states: "I will not regard [the Hindu deities] as gods nor will I worship them. . . . I embrace today the Buddha Dhamma discarding the Hindu religion which is detrimental to the emancipation of human beings and which believes in inequality and regards human beings other than Brahmins as low born" (Zelliot, p. 204).
8. See H. R. Isaacs, *India's Ex-Untouchables* (New York, 1965), pp. 90ff.
9. Wales, *op. cit.*, p. 66.
10. Cited by Smith, *Religion*, p. 84.
11. *Ibid.*, p. 96.

12. See E. Sarkisyanz, *Buddhist Backgrounds of the Burmese Revolution* (The Hague, 1965), chs. 22-23, on the Marxist and shamanistic influences.
13. See R. Butwell, *U Nu of Burma* (Stanford, 1963), especially pp. 61-71, on his Buddhist pietism.
14. Analogues with Marxist doctrine most often mentioned are: (1) no god or theory of creation, (2) atomic "materialism," (3) monastic rejection of personal ownership of property, etc. See Smith, *Religion*, pp. 125-136; cf. K. Chen, *Buddhism* (New York, 1968), pp. 269-275; E. Benz, *Buddhism or Communism?* (New York, 1960), F. Story, *Buddhism Answers the Marxist Challenge* (Rangoon, 1952).
15. See K. Wells, *Thailand* (Bangkok, 1946), introduction and chs. 1-2.
16. Cited in Smith, *Religion*, p. 292.
17. See Sarkisyanz, *op. cit.*, ch. 28, and postscript: "The existential tragedy of the Ashokan Buddhist political ideal is inherent in its aspiration to base the state on an ethical maximum, while the state by its very nature can only safeguard an ethical minimum. Yet without aspirations to transform morally political power, History's balance would be hopelessly gloomy indeed" (p. 236).
18. See Smith, *South Asian Politics*, chs. 21-22.
19. See N. Yalman's study of caste and kinship structures in Ceylon, *Under the Bo Tree* (Berkeley, 1967).
20. *Betrayal of Buddhism*, document of the All-India Buddhist Congress (Balangoda, 1956), pp. 100-101; and see E. R. Sarachandra, "The Case of Ceylon," in R. N. Bellah, *Religion and Progress in Modern Asia* (New York, 1965), pp. 109-123.
21. Cited by Smith, *South Asian Politics*, p. 477, n. 61.
22. See H. Welch, *The Buddhist Revival in China* (Cambridge, Mass., 1968), ch. 1.
23. *Ibid.*, chs. 3-7.
24. On the Buddhist apologists of this era (notably K'ang Yu-wei and Liang Ch'i-ch'ao), see *ibid.*, pp. 10-11, 115, 204-205; and Wright, *Buddhism*, pp. 111-113.
25. Wright, *Buddhism*, pp. 114, 122: "We are seeing, I believe, the last twilight of Buddhism as an organized religion." See C. K. Yang, *Religion in Chinese Society* (Berkeley, 1967), ch. 14. Cf. H. Welch, *The Practice of Chinese Buddhism* (Cambridge, Mass., 1967).
26. See G. C. Hickey, *Village in Vietnam* (Yale, 1964), ch. 3, for a description of current practices in one southern village.

27. J. Buttinger, *Vietnam: A Political History* (New York, 1968), pp. 61ff., 148ff. Thich Nat Hanh, *op. cit.*, pp. 14ff., 21ff.; G. Coulet, *Les Sociétés Secrétes en Terre d'Annam* (Saigon, 1925).

28. Hanh, *op. cit.*, pp. 41ff.

29. Buttinger, *op. cit.*, pp. 191ff.

30. Hanh, *op. cit.*, pp. 44ff.

31. J. Lacouture, *Vietnam: Between Two Truces* (New York, 1965), pp. 207ff.; B. Newman, *Background to Vietnam* (New York, 1966), pp. 151ff.; G. Kahin and J. Lewis, *The United States in Vietnam* (New York, 1967), ch. 7; M. Gettleman, *Vietnam* (New York, 1965), pp. 262ff.; Hanh, *op. cit.*, pp. 106ff. (on self-immolation); and M. Higgins, *Our Vietnam Nightmare* (New York, 1965).

32. Hanh, *op. cit.*, p. 45.

33. Ekvall, *op. cit.*, pp. 90-93; and T. J. Norbu (the Dalai Lama's brother), *Tibet Is My Country* (London, 1960).

34. See Anesaki, *History*, pp. 259ff., 334-337; deBary, *Sources of Japanese Tradition*, pp. 638ff.

35. R. N. Bellah, *Tokugawa Religion: The Values of Pre-industrial Japan* (Boston, 1970); and Bellah, "Reflections on the Protestant Ethic Analogy in Asia," in *Beyond Belief* (New York, 1970), pp. 53-63.

36. See H. N. McFarland, *The Rush Hour of the Gods* (New York, 1967); and B. Watanabe, "Modern Japanese Religions: Their Success Explained," *Monumenta Nipponica*, VIII (1957), 153-162.

37. J. D. Dator, *Sōka Gakkai, Builders of the Third Civilization* (Seattle, 1969); N. S. Brannen, *Sōka Gakkai* (Richmond, Va., 1968).

38. Brannen, *op. cit.*, pp. 110ff.; they oppose nuclear weapons, military treaties with the West, and urge "purification of the political world," tax cuts for the working and middle classes, social security, better housing, and amelioration of the traffic problem.

39. See their recent publication, *Risshō Kōseikai* (Tokyo, 1966).

40. Nishida (1870-1945), *The Problem of Japanese Culture*, in deBary, *op. cit.*, pp. 857-872; Kawakami (1879-1946), *Prison Ramblings*, in deBary, *op. cit.*, pp. 872ff.; his fusion of Marxism, Zen, and Pure Land resulted in his imprisonment. See Bellah, *Beyond Belief* (New York, 1970), pp. 108ff.

41. R. N. Bellah, "Ienaga Saburō and the Search for Meaning in Modern Japan," in M. E. Jansen (ed.), *Changing Japa-*

nese Attitudes towards Modernization (Princeton, 1965); and see Bellah, *Beyond Belief* (New York, 1970), ch. 7.

42. See R. Schwab, *La Renaissance orientale* (Paris, 1950).

43. H. Hesse, *Siddhartha* (New York, 1957); cf. Edwin Arnold's old classic *The Light of Asia* (Chicago, 1900); and John Masefield's *Gautama the Enlightened* (New York, 1941).

44. E. Fromm (ed.), *Zen Buddhism and Psychoanalysis* (New York, 1963); A. Watts, *Psychotherapy, East and West* (New York, 1961).

45. Striking contrasts are apparent in many areas, for example, the very different uses to which Timothy Leary and Thomas Merton have put Buddhist symbols: Leary has used selections from the *Tibetan Book of the Dead* as "inspirational" media for the psychedelic experience, while Merton sought inspiration for specifically moral values, particularly with regard to pacifist interests.

Selected Bibliography

CHINA

General Histories and Sources

deBary, T. W. (ed.). *Sources of the Chinese Tradition*. New York: Columbia University Press, 1950.

Chen, K. *Buddhism in China*. Princeton: Princeton University Press, 1964.

Maspero, H. *Mélanges posthumes sur les Religions et l'histoire de la Chine*. Paris: Civilisations du Sud, 1950.

Takakusu, J., and Watanabe, K. *Taishō shinshu Daizokyo* (Chinese Tripitaka), Taishō Issaikyo Kanko Kai, 85 vols. Tokyo, 1914-1932.

Weber, Max, *The Religion of China*. Glencoe, Ill.: Free Press, 1960.

Wright, Arthur. *Buddhism in Chinese History*. Stanford: Stanford University Press, 1959.

Yang, C. K. *Religion in Chinese Society*. Berkeley: University of California Press, 1967.

Zürcher, E. *The Buddhist Conquest of China*, 2 vols. Leiden: E. J. Brill, 1959.

Sects and Schools: doctrine and institutions

Bodde, Derk. "The Chinese View of Immortality; Its Expression by Chu Hsi and Its Relationship to Buddhist Thought," *Review of Religion*, 6 (1942), 369-83.

Chang, Carson. *The Development of Neo-Confucian Thought*, 2 vols. New York: Bookman Associates, 1957-1962.

Chang Chen-chi. *The Practice of Zen*. New York: Harper, 1959.

Demiéville, Paul, "La Pénétration du Bouddhisme dans la tradition philosophique chinoise," *Cahiers d'histoire mondiale*, III, 1 (1956), 19-38.

Dumoulin, H. *History of Zen Buddhism*. New York: Pantheon Books, 1963.

Fung Yu-lan, *History of Chinese Philosophy*, 2 vols. Princeton: Princeton University Press, 1952-1953.

Gernet, J. *Les aspects économiques du bouddhisme dans la*

société chinoise du Ve au Xe siècle. Saigon: École Française d'Extrême Orient, 1956.

Hurvitz, L. *Chih-i, in Mélanges Chinoise et Bouddhiques*, XII. Bruxelles; Bruges: 1962.

Reischauer, E. O. *Ennin's Travels in T'ang China*. New York: Ronald Press, 1955.

Suzuki, D. T., "The Development of the Pure Land Doctrine," *Eastern Buddhist*, 3, 285-327.

————. Essay on Hua-yen, in *Essays in Zen Buddhism*, 3rd Series. London: Rider, 1953.

Takakusu, J. *The Essentials of Buddhist Philosophy*. Honolulu: University of Hawaii Press, 1947.

Twitchett, D. W. "The Monasteries and China's Economy in Mediaeval Times," *Bulletin of the School of Oriental and African Studies*, 19, 3 (1957), 526-549.

————. "Monastic Estates in T'ang China," *Asia Major*, NS, 5 (1956), 123-146.

Yamakami Sogen. *Systems of Buddhist Thought*. Calcutta: Calcutta University Press, 1912.

Yampolsky, P. *The Platform Sutra of the Sixth Patriarch*. New York: Columbia University Press, 1967.

Waley, Arthur. *The Real Tripitaka* (*Hsuan-tsang*). London: Allen & Unwin, 1952.

Wright, A. F. "The Formation of Sui Ideology," in John Fairbank (ed.), *Chinese Thought and Institutions*, pp. 93-104. Chicago: Chicago University Press, 1957.

Contemporary Studies

Chan Wing-tsit. *Religious Trends in Modern China*. New York: Columbia University Press, 1953.

Welch, Holmes. *The Buddhist Revival in China*. Cambridge: Harvard University Press, 1968.

————. *The Practice of Chinese Buddhism*. Cambridge: Harvard University Press, 1967.

Ceylon and India

CEYLON

General Histories and Sources

Arasaratnam, S. *Ceylon*. Englewood Cliffs, N.J.: Prentice Hall, 1964.

Bechert, H. *Buddhismus, Staat und Gesellschaft in den Laen-
dern des Theravada Buddhismus,* 2 vols. Frankfurt am
Main: A. Metzner, 1966-1967.

Geiger, W. *Culture of Ceylon in Medieval Times.* Wiesbaden:
Harrassowitz, 1960.

Geiger, W. (trans.). *Mahavamsa: The Great Chronicle of Ceylon.* London: Luzac, 1964.

Lamotte, E. *Histoire du Bouddhisme Indien,* pp. 129-135, 291-
298, 320-387, 395-406, 534-536. Louvain: Publications
Universitaires, 1958.

Mendis, G. C. *Ceylon Today and Yesterday.* Colombo: Associated Newspapers of Ceylon, 1957.

Oldenberg, H. *The Dipavamsa, an Ancient Buddhist Historical
Record.* London: Williams and Norgate, 1879.

Rahula, W. *History of Buddhism in Ceylon.* Colombo: Gunasena, 1966.

Contemporary Issues

Ames, Michael M. "Buddha and the Dancing Goblins." *American Anthropologist,* 66 (1964), 75-82.

———. "Magical-Animism and Buddhism: A Structural Analysis of the Sinhalese Religious System," *Journal of American Sociology,* 23 (1964), 21-52.

The Betrayal of Buddhism. Balagoda: Dharmavijaya Press,
1956.

Ryan, Bryce. *Caste in Modern Ceylon.* New Brunswick: Rutgers
University Press, 1953.

Smith, Donald E. (ed.). *South Asian Politics and Religion,* pp.
451-546. Princeton: Princeton University Press, 1969.

Vijayavardhana, D. C. *Dharma-Vijaya.* Colombo: Sinha Publications, 1953.

Vimalananda, T. *Buddhism in Ceylon under the Christian
Powers.* Colombo: Gunasena and Co., 1963.

Vittachi, Tarzie. *Emergency '58: The Story of the Ceylon Race
Riots.* London: Deutsch, 1958.

Wriggins, W. H. *Ceylon: Dilemmas of a New Nation.* Princeton:
Princeton University Press, 1960.

Yalman, N. *Under the Bo Tree.* Berkeley: University of California Press, 1967.

INDIA

General Histories and Sources

deBary, T. W. (ed.). *Sources of the Indian Traditions*. New York: Columbia University Press, 1960.

Conzé, E. (ed.). *Buddhist Texts through the Ages*. New York: Harper Torchbook, 1964.

———. *Buddhist Thought in India*. London: Allen & Unwin, 1962; also available in Harper Torchbook series.

———. *Thirty Years of Buddhist Studies*. Oxford: Cassirer, 1967.

Lamotte, Étienne. *Histoire du Bouddhisme Indien*. Paris: Publications Universitaires, 1958.

Renou, L. and Filliozat, J. *L'Inde Classique*, Vol. I., Paris: Payot, 1947; Vol. II, Paris: Imprimerie Nationale, 1953.

Thomas, E. J. *History of Buddhist Thought*. London: Routledge & Kegan Paul, 1951.

Weber, M. *The Religion of India*. Glencoe, Ill.: Free Press, 1958.

Winternitz, M. Vol. 2 of *History of Indian Literature*, 2 vols. Calcutta: Calcutta University Press, 1933.

Early Buddhism: literature, doctrine, institutions

Bareau, A. *Les Sectes bouddhiques du Petit Véhicule*. Saigon: École Française d'Extrême-Orient, 1955.

Dutt, N. *Early Monastic Buddhism*, 2 vols. Calcutta: Calcutta University Press, 1941-1945.

Dutt, S. *Early Buddhist Monachism*. London: Kegan Paul, 1924.

———. *Early History of the Spread of Buddhism and the Buddhist Schools*. London: Luzac, 1925.

Foucher, A. *La Vie du Buddha*. Paris: Payot, 1949.

Geiger, W. *Pāli Dhamma*. Munich: Bayerischen Akademie, 1920.

———. *Pāli Literature and Language*. Calcutta: Calcutta University Press, 1956.

Guenther, H. *Philosophy and Psychology in the Abhidhamma*. Lucknow: Buddha Vihara, 1957.

Jayatilleke, K. N. *Early Buddhist Theory of Knowledge*. London: Allen & Unwin, 1963.

Law, B. C. *The Buddhist Conception of Spirits*. London: Luzac, 1936.

————. *History of Pāli Literature.* 2 vols. London: Kegan Paul, 1933.

Masson, Joseph. *La Religion populaire dans le canon boud-dhique Pāli.* Louvain, Bureaux du Muséon, 1942.

Poussin, L. de La Vallée. *L'Abhidharmakośa de Vasubandhu.* Paris: Geuthner, 1923-1931.

Stcherbatsky, T. *The Central Conception of Buddhism.* Calcutta: Gupta, 1956.

————. *Conception of Buddhist Nirvāṇa.* Leningrad: Office of the Academy of Sciences of the U.S.S.R., 1927.

Thomas, E. J. *Life of the Buddha as Legend and History.* London: Routledge & Kegan Paul, 1927.

Warren, H. C. *Buddhism in Translations.* Cambridge: Harvard University Press, 1896.

Mahāyāna

Chatterjee, Ashok. *Yogacara Idealism.* Benares: University Press, 1962.

Conze, E. *Buddhist Wisdom Books* (Diamond-Cutter and Heart Sūtras). London: Allen & Unwin, 1958.

————. "The Ontology of the Prajñāpāramitā," *Philosophy East and West,* 3, 2 (1953), 117-130.

————. *Selected Sayings from the Perfection of Wisdom.* London: Buddhist Society, 1955.

Dayal, Har. *The Bodhisattva Doctrine in Buddhist Sanskrit Literature.* London: Kegan Paul, 1932.

Dutt, N. *Aspects of Mahāyāna Buddhism and its Relations to Hīnayāna.* London: Luzac, 1930.

Hirakawa, Akira. "The Rise of Mahāyāna Buddhism and Its Relationship to the Worship of Stupas," *Memoirs of the Research Department of the Toyo Bunko No. 22* (1963), pp. 57-106.

Kern, H. (trans.). *The Saddharma-puṇḍarīka or the Lotus of the True Law,* in F. M. Müller (ed.), *Sacred Books of the East,* Vol. 21. Oxford: Clarendon Press, 1909.

Lamotte, É. *L'Enseignement de Vimalakīrti.* Louvain: Publications Universitaires, 1962.

————. *La Somme du Grand Véhicule d'Asaṅga* (Mahāyāna-saṃgraha), 2 vols. Louvain: Bureaux du Muséon, 1938.

de Mallmann, M. T. *Introduction a l'étude d'Avalokitiçvara.* Paris: Civilisations du Sud, 1948.

Müller, F. M. (trans.). (1) *The Larger Sukhāvatī-vyūha.* (2)

The Smaller Sukhāvatī-vyūha (Pure Land Sūtras), in F. M. Müller (ed.), *Sacred Books of the East*, Vol. 49. Oxford: Clarendon Press, 1909.

Murti, T. R. V. *Central Philosophy of Buddhism.* London: Allen & Unwin, 1955.

Robinson, Richard H. *Classical Indian Philosophy.* Madison, Wis.: College Printing and Typing, 1968.

Streng, F. J. *Emptiness: A Study in Religious Meaning.* Nashville: Abingdon Press, 1967.

Suzuki, D. T. *Açvagosha's Discourse on the Awakening of Faith in Mahāyāna.* Chicago: Open Court, 1900.

————. *The Laṅkāvatāra Sūtra.* London: Kegan Paul, 1956.

————. *Studies in the Laṅkāvatāra Sūtra.* London: Routledge and Sons, 1930.

Tantrayāna

Bagchi, P. C. *Studies in the Tantras.* Calcutta: Calcutta University Press, 1939.

Bharati, A. *The Tantric Tradition.* London: Rider, 1965.

Bhattacharya, B. *An Introduction to Buddhist Esotericism.* London: Oxford University Press, 1932.

Dasgupta, S. B. *An Introduction to Tantric Buddhism.* Calcutta: Calcutta University Press, 1950.

————. *Obscure Religious Cults.* Calcutta: Calcutta University Press, 1946.

Eliade, M. *Yoga: Immortality and Freedom.* Princeton: Princeton University Press, 1970.

Shahidullah, M. (ed. and trans.). *Les chants mystique de Kāṇha et de Saraha.* Paris, 1928. (Reprinted and edited by L. Misch, Library of Congress, Washington, D.C., 1958.)

Snellgrove, D. L. *The Hevajra Tantra*, 2 vols. London: Oxford University Press, 1959.

Social and Political Teachings

Ambedkar, B. R. "Le Buddha et l'avenir du Buddhisme," in R. de Berval (ed.), *Présence du Bouddhisme*, France-Asie, Vol. XVI, Saigon (Feb.-June, 1959).

————. *What Congress and Gandhi Have Done to the Untouchables.* Bombay: Thacker and Co., 1946.

Bloch, J. *Les Inscriptions d'Asoka.* Paris: Société d'édition, 1950.

Drekmeier, C. *Kingship and Community in Early India*. Stanford: Stanford University Press, 1962.

Eggermont, P. H. L. *The Chronology of the Reign of Asoka Moriya*. Leiden: E. J. Brill, 1956.

Fick, R. *The Social Organization in Northeast India in the Buddha's Time*. Calcutta: Calcutta University Press, 1920.

Gokhale, B. G. "Dhammiko Dhammaraja: A Study in Buddhist Constitutional Concepts," *Indica*, Silver Jubilee Commemorative Volume (1953).

———. "Early Buddhist View of the State," *Journal of the American Oriental Society*, LXXXIX, No. 4 (1969).

Horner, I. B. *Women under Primitive Buddhism*. London: Routledge and Sons, 1930.

Isaacs, H. R. *India's Ex-Untouchables*, New York: Asia Publishing House, 1965.

Keer, D. *Dr. Ambedkar, Life and Mission*. Bombay: Popular Prakashan, 1962.

King, Winston K. *In the Hope of Nibbāna: an Essay on Theravāda Buddhist Ethics*. La Salle, Ill.: Open Court, 1964.

Kosambi, D. D. *Ancient India*. New York: Pantheon Books, 1965.

———. *Introduction to the Study of Indian History*. Bombay: Popular Book Depot, 1956.

Malalasekera, G. P. *Buddhism and the Race Question*. Paris, Publications, 1958.

Przyluski, J. *La Légende de l'empereur Açoka*, Annales du Musée Guimet, Bibliothèque d'Études, Tome 31. Paris: Geuthner, 1923.

Robinson, Richard H. "The Religion of the Householder Bodhisattva," in *Bhārati*, (Benares, 1966), pp. 31-55.

Smith, Donald D. *India as a Secular State*. Princeton: Princeton University Press, 1963.

Tachibana, S. *The Ethics of Buddhism*. London: Oxford University Press, 1926.

Thapar, Romila. *Asoka and the Decline of the Mauryas*. London: Oxford University Press, 1961.

Zelliot, E. "Buddhism and Politics in Maharashtra," in D. E. Smith (ed.), *South Asia Politics and Religion*, pp. 191-212. Princeton: Princeton University Press, 1969.

JAPAN

General Histories and Sources

Anesaki, M. *History of Japanese Religion.* Tokyo: Charles Tuttle and Co., 1963.

Aston, G. W. *Chronicles of Japan,* 2 vols. London: Kegan Paul, 1896.

Bando, Shojun, *et al. A Bibliography on Japanese Buddhism.* Tokyo: Cultural Exchange Institute, 1958.

deBary, W. T. (ed.), *Sources of the Japanese Tradition.* New York: Columbia University Press, 1960.

Bunce, W. *Religions of Japan.* Rutland, Vermont: Charles Tuttle and Co., 1955.

Eliot, Charles. *Japanese Buddhism.* London: New York: Barnes & Noble, 1959.

Kidder, J. E. *Japan before Buddhism.* London: Thames and Hudson, 1959.

Kitagawa, J. M. "The Buddhist Transformation in Japan," *History of Religions,* IV (1965), 319-336.

————. *Religion in Japanese History.* New York: Columbia University Press, 1960.

————. "The Religions of Japan," in C. J. Adams (ed.), *A Reader's Guide to the Great Religions.* New York: Free Press, 1965.

Nakamura, H. *Ways of Thinking of Eastern Peoples.* Honolulu: East-West Center Press, 1964.

Sansom, G. *Japan: A Short Cultural History.* New York: Appleton-Century-Crofts, 1943.

Saunders, E. D. *Buddhism in Japan.* Philadelphia: University of Pennsylvania Press, 1964.

de Visser, M. W. *Ancient Buddhism in Japan.* Paris: Geuthner, 1928-1935.

Schools and Sects

Anesaki, M. *Nichiren, the Buddhist Prophet.* Cambridge: Harvard University Press, 1916.

Bloom, Alfred. *Shinran's Gospel of Pure Grace.* Tucson: University of Arizona Press, 1965.

Coates, H. W., and Ishizuaka, R. *Hōnen, the Buddhist Saint.* Tokyo: Kodokaku, 1930.

Kitagawa, J. M. "Master and Saviour," *Studies of Esoteric Buddhism and Tantrism*, pp. 1-26. Koyasan: University Press, 1965.

Lloyd, Arthur. *The Creed of Half Japan*. London: Smith, Elder, 1911.

———. *Shinran and His Work*. Tokyo: Kyobunkwah, 1910.

Masutani, F., and Yoshimichi, U. "Buddhism," in H. Kishimoto (ed.), *Japanese Religion in the Meiji Era* (trans. J. F. Howes) pp. 99-169. Tokyo: Obunsha, 1956.

Steinilber-Oberlin, E., and Matsuo, K. *The Buddhist Sects of Japan*. London: Allen & Unwin, 1938.

Suzuki, D. T. *Zen and Japanese Culture*. New York: Pantheon, 1959.

Tajima, R. *Les deux grands maṇḍalas et la doctrine de l'esoterisme Shingon*. Paris: Presses Universitaires de France, 1959.

Contemporary

Bellah, R. N. "Ienaga Saburo and the Search for Meaning in Modern Japan," in M. E. Jensen (ed.). *Changing Japanese Attitudes towards Modernization*. Princeton: Princeton University Press, 1965.

———. *Beyond Belief*. New York: Harper, 1970.

———. (ed.) *Religion and Progress in Modern Asia*. New York: Free Press, 1965.

———. *Tokugawa Religion*. Boston: Beacon Press, 1970.

Brannen, N. S. *Sōka Gakkai*, Richmond, Va.: John Knox Press, 1968.

Dator, J. D. *Sōka Gakkai, Builders of the Third Civilization*. Seattle: University of Washington Press, 1969.

Kapleau, Philip. *The Three Pillars of Zen*. New York: Harper, 1966.

McFarland, H. N. *The Rush Hour of the Gods: A Study of the New Religious Movements in Japan*. New York: Macmillan, 1967.

Schiffer, Wilhelm. "New Religions in Postwar Japan," *Monumenta Nipponica*, XI (1955), 1-14.

Thomsen, Harry. *Bibliography on the New Religions*. Kyoto: The Christian Center, 1960.

Tsukamoto, Z. "Japanese and Chinese Buddhism," G. S. Metraux and F. Crouzet (eds.), in *Religions and the Prom-*

ise of the Twentieth Century. New York: New American Library, 1965.

Watanabe, S. *Japanese Buddhism: A Critical Appraisal,* trans. A. Bloom. Tokyo: Kokusai Bunka Shinkokai, 1964.

SOUTHEAST ASIA

General Histories

Cady, J. F. *Thailand, Burma, Laos and Cambodia.* Englewood Cliffs, N.J.: Prentice-Hall, 1966.

Coedès, George. *Histoire ancienne des états hindouises d'Extrême-Orient.* Hanoi: Imprimerie d'Extrême-Orient, 1944; Paris, 1964.

————. *The Making of South East Asia.* Berkeley: University of California Press, 1967.

Groslier, B. P. *The Art of Indochina.* New York: Crown, 1962.

Hall, D. G. E. *A History of South-East Asia.* New York: Macmillan, 1968.

Harrison, Brian. *Southeast Asia.* London: Macmillan, 1954.

Heine-Geldern, R. von. *Conceptions of State and Kingship in Southeast Asia.* Southeast Asia Program Data Paper No. 18. Ithaca, N.Y.: Cornell University Press, 1963.

Landon, Kenneth P. *Southeast Asia: Crossroad of Religions.* Chicago: University of Chicago Press, 1949.

LeMay, R. S. *The Culture of South-East Asia: The Heritage of India.* London: Allen & Unwin, 1954.

Malleret, Louis. *Pour comprendre la sculpture buddhique et brahmanique en Indochine.* Saigon: Portail, 1942.

Maspero, Georges. *L'Indochine,* 2 vols. Paris: G. Van Oest, 1929.

Migot, O. "Le Bouddhisme en Général," *Bulletin de la Société des Études Indo-chinoises* (Saigon), XXI (1946), 29-41.

————. "Le Bouddhisme en Indo Chine," *Bulletin de la Société des Études Indo-chinoises* (Saigon), XXII (1947), 23-29.

Burma

Butwell, R. *U Nu of Burma.* Stanford: Stanford University Press, 1963.

Cady, John F. *A History of Modern Burma.* Ithaca, N.Y.: Cornell University Press, 1958.

Harvey, G. E. *Outline of Burmese History*. Calcutta: Longmans, Green, 1947.

King, W. L. *A Thousand Lives Away: Buddhism in Contemporary Burma*. Cambridge, Mass.: Harvard University Press, 1964.

Maung Htin Aung. *Folk Elements in Burmese Buddhism*. London: Oxford University Press, 1962.

Mya Maung. "Cultural Value and Economic Change in Burma," *Asian Survey*, IV (1964), 757-64.

Nash, M. "Burmese Buddhism in Everyday Life," *American Anthropologist*, 65 (1963), 285-295.

Pye, L. W. *Politics, Personality and Nation Building: Burma's Search for Identity*. New Haven: Yale University Press, 1962.

Ray, N. R. *Theravāda Buddhism in Burma*. Calcutta: Calcutta University Press, 1946.

Sarkisyanz, E. *Buddhist Backgrounds of the Burmese Revolution*. The Hague: Martinus Nijhoff, 1965.

Smith, Donald E. *Religion and Politics in Burma*. Princeton: Princeton University Press, 1965.

Spiro, M. E. *Burmese Supernaturalism*. Englewood Cliffs, N.J.: Prentice-Hall, 1967.

Totten, George O. (ed.). "Buddhism and Socialism in Japan and Burma," *Comparative Studies in Society and History*, Vol. 2 (1960).

U Ba Swe, *The Burmese Revolution*. Rangoon: Ministry of Information, Union of Burma, 1952.

Cambodia and Laos

Briggs, Lawrence P. *The Ancient Khmer Empire*. Philadelphia: American Philosophical Society, 1951.

Brodrick, Alan H. *Little Vehicle: Cambodia and Laos*. London: Hutchinson, 1949.

Chatterji, B. R. *Indian Cultural Influence in Cambodia*. Calcutta: Calcutta University Press, 1928.

Coedès, George. "Documents sur l'histoire politique et religieuse du Laos occidental," *Bulletin de l'École Française d'Extrême-Orient*, Vol. 25 (1925).

————. *Pour mieux comprendre Angkor*. Hanoi: Imprimerie d'Extrême-Orient, 1943.

Glaize, Maurice. *Les Monuments du groupe d'Angkor*. Saigon: Portail, 1944.

Halpern, J. M. *Government, Politics and Social Structure in Laos*. Monograph Series No. 4. Southeast Asia Studies, Yale University, 1965.

LeBar, R. M. and Suddard, A. (eds.). *Laos*. New Haven: Human Relations Area File, 1960.

Leclere, Adhemard. *Cambodige: Fêtes Civiles et Religieuses*. Paris, 1916.

Maspero, Georges. *La Royaume de Champa*. Paris: G. Van Oest, 1928.

Poree, G. and Maspero, E. *Cérémonies des Douze Mois*. Pnompenh: Commission des Moeurs, 1950.

Steinberg, D. J. (ed.). *Cambodia: Its People, Its Society, Its Culture*. New Haven: Human Relations Area File, 1959.

Upasaka, Purusakara. "Le Peuple Cambodgien Est Plus Buddhique que ses Bonzes," *Indochine Sud-Est Asiatique*, XXXI (July 1954), 25-31.

Indonesia and Malaya

Damais, L. C. "Le Bouddhisme en Indonésie," in R. de Berval (ed.), *Présence du Bouddhisme*. Saigon, 1959.

Devattuti, D. *India and Ancient Malaya*. Singapore: Eastern University Presses, 1965.

Geertz, Clifford. *The Religion of Java*. Glencoe. Ill.: Free Press, 1960.

Krom, N. J. *Barabudar, Archeological Description*, 2 vols. The Hague: Martinus Nijhoff, 1927.

Mus, Paul. *Barabudur*, 2 vols. Hanoi: Imprimerie d'Extrême-Orient, 1935.

Naerssen, F. H. van. *Culture Contacts and Social Conflicts in Indonesia*. New York: Southeast Asia Institute, 1947.

Winstedt, R. O. *The Malays—A Cultural History*. London: Routledge, Kegan Paul, 1958.

Thailand

Blanchard, Wendell (*et al.*). *Thailand, Its People, Its Society, Its Culture*. New Haven: Human Relations Area File, 1958.

Coedès, George (ed. and trans.). *Récueil des inscriptions du Siam*, 2 vols. Bangkok: Bangkok Times Press, 1924-1929.

Graham, W. A. *Siam*, 2 vols. London: Alexander Moring, 1924.

Landon, Kenneth P. *Siam in Transition.* Chicago: University of Chicago Press, 1939.

LeMay, Reginald M. *Buddhist Art in Siam.* Cambridge: University Press, 1938.

Moffat, Abbot L. *Mongkut: The King of Siam.* Ithaca, N.Y.: Cornell University Press, 1961.

Pfanner, D. E. and Ingersoll. "Theravāda Buddhism and Village Economic Behavior: A Burmese and Thai Comparison," *Journal of Asian Studies,* Vol. 21 (1962).

Rajadhon, Phya A. *Life and Ritual in Old Siam.* New Haven: Human Relations Area File, 1961.

Seidenfaden, Erik. *The Thai Peoples.* Bangkok: Siam Society, 1958.

Vella, Walter F. *Siam under Rama III.* Locust Valley, N.Y.: Augustin, 1957.

Wales, H. G. Quaritch. *Ancient Siamese Government and Administration.* London: Bernard Quaritch, 1934.

———. *Siamese State Ceremonies.* London: Bernard Quaritch, 1931.

Wells, K. E. *Thai Buddhism, Its Rites and Activities.* Bangkok: Bangkok Times Press, 1939.

de Young, J. *Village Life in Modern Thailand.* Berkeley: University of California Press, 1955.

Vietnam

Buttinger, J. M. Vietnam: *A Political History.* New York: Praeger, 1968.

Cadière, Léopold. *Croyances et practiques religieuses des Annamites.* Hanoi: Imprimerie d'Extrême-Orient, 1944.

Gettleman, M. E. (ed.). *Vietnam.* New York: Fawcett, 1969.

Hickey, G. C. *Village in Vietnam.* New Haven: Yale University Press, 1964.

Higgins, Marguerite. *Our Vietnam Nightmare.* New York: Harper, 1965.

Kahin, G. B., and Lewis, J. W. *The United States in Vietnam.* New York: Dial, 1967.

Lacouture, Jean. *Vietnam between Two Truces.* New York: Vintage, 1966.

Newman, Bernard. *Background to Vietnam.* New York: Signet, 1966.

Nguyen Van Luyen. *Le Viet-Nam.* Hanoi: Le-Van-Phue, 1945.

TIBET

General Histories and Sources

Hoffman, Helmut. *The Religions of Tibet.* New York: Macmillan, 1961.

Norbu, T. J. *Tibet Is My Country.* London: Rupert Hart-Davis, 1960.

Norbu, T. J., and Turnbull, C. M. *Tibet.* New York: Simon and Schuster, 1968.

Obermiller, E. (trans.). *History of Buddhism* (of Bu-ston), in two parts. Heidelberg: O. Harrassowitz, 1931-1932.

Pelliot, Paul. *Histoire ancienne du Tibet.* Paris: Librarie d'Amérique et d'Orient, 1961.

Shen, T. L., and Liu, S. C. *Tibet and Tibetans.* Stanford: Stanford University Press, 1953.

Snellgrove, David L. *The Nine Ways of Bon.* London: Oxford University Press, 1967.

Snellgrove, David L., and Richardson, H. *A Cultural History of Tibet.* New York: Praeger, 1968.

Stein, R. A. *La civilisation tibétaine.* Paris: Dunod, 1962.

Thomas, F. W. *Ancient Folk-Literature from North Eastern Tibet.* Berlin: Akademie-Verlag, 1957.

———. *Tibetan Literary Texts and Documents concerning Chinese Turkestan,* 3 vols. London: Royal Asiatic Society, 1935-1955.

Religious Sects, Personalities, and Practices

Bacot, J. *Le poète tibétain Milarépa.* Paris: Editions Bossard, 1925.

———. *La vie de Marpa le "traducteur."* Paris: Librarie Orientaliste, Paul Geuthner, 1937.

Bell, Charles. *Portrait of the Dalai Lama.* London: Collins, 1946.

Blofield, John. *The Tantric Mysticism of Tibet.* New York: Dutton, 1970.

Carrasco, Pedro. *Land and Polity in Tibet.* Seattle: University of Washington Press, 1959.

Chattopadhyaya, A. *Atiśa and Tibet.* Calcutta: R. D. Press, 1967.

Dawson, C. H. *The Mongol Mission.* New York: Sheed & Ward, 1955.

Demiéville, Paul. *Le Concile de Lhasa.* Paris: Imprimerie Nationale de France, 1952.

Ekvall, R. E. *Religious Observances in Tibet: Patterns and Function.* Chicago: University of Chicago Press, 1964.

Evans-Wentz, W. Y. *The Tibetan Book of the Dead.* London: Oxford University Press, 1960.

———. *The Tibetan Book of the Great Liberation.* London: Oxford University Press, 1969.

———. *Tibet's Great Yogi Milarepa.* London: Oxford University Press, 1951.

Gordan, Antoinette K. *The Hundred Thousand Songs: Selections from Milarepa, Poet-Saint of Tibet.* Rutland, Vermont: Charles Tuttle and Co., 1961.

Hoffman, Helmut. *Mi-la Ras-pa, Sieben Legenden.* Munich, 1950.

———. *Quellen zur Geschichte der tibetischen Bon-Religion.* Wiesbaden: F. Steiner, 1950.

Miller, Robert J. *Monasteries and Culture Change in Inner Mongolia.* Wiesbaden: O. Harrassowitz, 1959.

Nebesky-Wojikowitz, R. *Oracles and Demons of Tibet.* The Hague: Mouton, 1956.

Obermiller, E. *Tsong-kha-pa le Pandit,* in *Mélanges chinois et bouddhique,* Vol. III, p. 319. Brussels, 1935.

Stein, R. A. *L'épopée tibétain de Gésar.* Paris: Presses Universitaires de France, 1956.

Toussaint, G. C. *Le dict de Padma.* Paris: E. Leroux, 1933.

Tucci, G. *Tibetan Painted Scrolls.* 2 vols. Rome: La Libreria dello Stato, 1949.

———. *To Lhasa and Beyond.* Rome: Instituto Poligrafico dello Stato, 1956.

Index

A

Abhayagiri monastery, 87, 88
Abhidhamma, 23, 83
Ādibuddha, 50, 111
Ahiṃsā, 29, 145
Ai, 64
Altan Khan, 111
Ambedkar, B. R., 138ff.
Amitābha (Amita, Amida),
  42, 62, 67, 72, 73, 111,
  126ff.
Anattā, 9, 11, 12, 15, 42
Anawrahta, 92
Angkor, 91, 95, 97
Anglicanism, 147
Anicca, 9
Arhat, 34, 35
Art and Architecture, 33, 40,
  49, 71, 78, 97, 133
Ārvadeva, 48
Aryan civilization, 2–6
Ashikaga Shogunate, 132, 134
Aśoka, 31ff., 68, 82, 83, 92,
  95, 138
Atīśa, 105, 106, 108, 109
Ātman, 4
Authority, problem of, 23–27,
  32, 63, 64, 65, 66, 67, 74–
  77, 82, 83, 118, 119, 120,
  121, 124, 125, 131, 134,
  142, 145, 146, 150, 151

Avalokiteśvara (Kuan-yin), 72,
  105, 111, 113
Avataṃsaka Sūtra, 70, 71, 119
Avijjā, 9
Āyurvedic medicine, 150

B

Bandaranaike, S. W., 149, 150
Betrayal of Buddhism, 148
Bodhi, 8
Bodhidharma, 74
Bodhisattva, 35, 36, 37, 39,
  40, 58, 72
Bönism, 98ff.
Borobudur, 97
Brahman, 16
Brāhmanism, 82, 90, 91, 140
Brāhman priests, 2, 85, 90, 94
Brom-ston, 105
Buddha, Siddhārtha Gautama,
  vii, 2, 6ff., 11, 26, 35
Buddha and His Dhamma,
  140
Buddhaghosa, 88
Buddharāja, 91
Buddhist Association of China,
  154
Bureaucracy, 24, 26, 63, 64,
  82ff., 89, 94, 96
Burma, 22, 89ff., 142ff.
Bushidō, 135, 158